CHOOSE BLISS

The Power and Practice
of Joy and Contentment

CHOOSE BLISS
The Power and Practice
of Joy and Contentment

Moneeka Sawyer

Inner Light Press
a Silver Torch Press company
Beverly Hills, 90210

Choose Bliss: The Power and Practice of Joy and Contentment

Copyright © 2016 by Moneeka Sawyer

www.CoreBlissLife.com

Published by Inner Light Press, a Silver Torch Press company
Beverly Hills, CA 90210
www.SilverTorchPress.com

ISBN 978-1-942707-28-8

Cover design by David T. Fagan and Katie Benedikt

Printed in the United State of America.

Dedication

This book is dedicated to my loving husband, David, and my amazing parents, Vishin and Vinita. I have been so blessed to have you as my teachers and role models for how to live a blissful life. Thank you for all your endless love and support. I couldn't have gotten this book out into the world without you. I love you.

Acknowledgments

I am so grateful for all the help and support I have gotten in creating this book. A project like this requires a village to be successful. I'd like to personally thank the following:

My publisher, Jill Fagan. Without you, this project never would have even gotten off the ground. Thank you for all your help and for being such a pleasure to work with.

My editor, Bonnie Hearn Hill. Without you, this would just be a compilation of badly worded sentences. Thanks for all the amazingly hard work you did to make my book what it is today.

David and Barry. Thank you for the many hours you spent with me, sitting at computers side-by-side, editing this book over and over again. And also for the many cups of coffee you each served me while I was writing.

Thank you, Dr. James Key, the master storyteller, for pulling my story out of me and helping me to shape it so it represents me perfectly.

Thank you, Pam and Ellie, for your undying support in this project and your endless patience as I worked through what I wanted to say.

Thank you to my sisters Neelam and Roini, for helping me work through the wealth of knowledge we all share to pick out the gems that are now in this book.

Thank you to Sonal, Janice, and Sian for your constant support and your encouragement to keep going when all I wanted to do was give up. Thank you, Emily Letran, for helping me get the cover I really wanted instead of settling for something that would be "fine."

Thank you to Toni Cay Snyder, Caterina Rando, Alison Douglas, Kay Ferguson, Jaimie Harnagel, and Benedict Pedro for your consistent encouragement and constant validation of how important it was to write this book.

Thank you, Dr. Andrew Wu, my acupuncturist, for the decades of support you've given me. I literally couldn't stand in my power today without you!

To JeAnna Weisand, thank you so much for keeping my office and creative spaces organized and beautiful so I could focus on writing and creating.

And thank you, Joseph Ghabi for your kind but firm mentoring that has brought me where I am today. And for the lovely foreword you wrote for me.

To Mom and Dad. Thank you for all you taught me so that I could write this book.

There are countless others of you that I would like to thank personally. Know that I am so very grateful for your help and support. You have made this project easier to work through, and you make my life a much more blissful one.

Table of Contents

Foreword

As a Blueprint Numerologist for over twenty years and concentrating on Psychosomatic Numerology, I've realized certain facts from encountering thousands of clients. We are all here to have freedom and personal responsibility in life in order to have happy, joyful, and fulfilled lives. We can be happy or joyful in one area or two, but miserable in other areas, so achieving the level of fulfillment we all seek can be difficult. But at the same time, it is completely attainable. As a reality check, we always need to ask ourselves how fulfilled we are in all areas of our lives—health, relationships, finances, sexuality and environment. Once we balance these areas, that will lead us into a state of love for everything we have in our environment, and we can live in peace and harmony.

It's all about energy! Everything around us is energy. Energy vibrates in different frequencies that can be either negative or positive, and we can find these frequencies in the choice of words we normally use on a daily basis, in the way we think, our thoughts, and in the way we speak. In order to have the peace you are looking for, you need to learn to choose the right words each day. Words have energy, and we usually label them as being negative or positive. Either way, you will invest the same amount of energy, so choose wisely!

I met Moneeka at an event in San Diego in 2013, and we had an instant connection. Soon after, I became her mentor. I continually found Moneeka a very magnetic and energetic person. She always laughs, and you can see and feel the joy in her. She is compassionate toward everything she touches, and she's always striving to bring balance to what's inside and out. You can feel she is alive and happy. I guess, looking at it now, she is in her state of bliss. I believe she is rightfully equipped to guide you through the hurdles that might be in your way today. She will walk through all the channels or obstacles that might be in your way to enlighten you so that you will be able to see life from a new perspective and have a brighter view about yourself, the people around you, and the Destiny you signed up for in this lifetime.

Bliss equates to peace and is even above the state of love. Moneeka's book will give you the proper tools to walk through the process in order to live the state of bliss. Bliss is available to all of us. She empowers people to take all the necessary steps to reach bliss and equilibrium in their life. I see Moneeka as a great coach who can lead you in the school of life. She is conscious, intelligent, and passionate, and she's committed to assisting every person who crosses her path to bring change into their lives. Moneeka provides us with tools that we can use whenever life presents new challenges and requires a new change of direction. She shows us the way to the direct elevator to find our own bliss.

It is your birthright to be happy, joyful, and fulfilled in life, and this is possible if you allow change to take place in your heart. Get ready to have a blissful life. You owe it to yourself!

In Light & Love!
Joseph Ghabi

Prologue

This book is about your power to choose.

It's about your power to choose not anxiety, not regret, not anger—but *bliss*.

When I awake every morning I choose again to marry my husband. I choose to continue to do this work that I love. I choose to be grateful and focus on what is good in the world.

And each morning, again and again, I choose bliss. So can you.

In order to make that choice and actually live it, I first needed to discover what bliss really was for me. Then, I needed to empower myself so I could live my life on my terms, no matter what anyone else said. And now, every single day, I need to embody this choice.

As a tool to help me do this, I often refer to a journal I started a long time ago. The most important entries in that journal came on the days, weeks, and months that I had the hardest time living in alignment with my bliss. During those times, I wrote down all the techniques I tried, and I discovered the ones that really worked. Over time, I developed a type of tool kit that I could turn to for tips that I could use to quickly bring myself back into a state of bliss, regardless of what was challenging me.

Once I had the tools for success, I often recommended them to my coaching clients, and they reported success after success in using the same tools. All of those experiences and all that I learned have become this book in the hopes that you can now step into your own bliss. That is why I wrote this book. I so want this for you.

I've organized the chapters to help you go through the process I went through to get to where I am today. First, you will discover and define what bliss really means to you. Then, you will learn tools to empower yourself with the strength to go after your bliss. Finally, I will show you some simple, immediately implementable ways to embody bliss in your life.

First, though, I'd like to share with you part of my story, the journey that led me from making other choices that didn't serve me well, choices that—in many ways—invited misery instead of happiness. This journey led me into the newfound joy and freedom that I currently experience each and every day.

It is my deepest hope that my story will inspire you to reconsider your own journey, to learn from where I've been, and above all, to *choose bliss*.

What is Bliss?

I define bliss as a state of absolute emotional contentment. It's a place of being in which there is always an underlying feeling of joy, satisfaction, and peace. It doesn't mean that life doesn't still continue to happen.

Things still go wrong. We still get hurt or feel sad, angry, or scared. But if we are living in a state of bliss, no matter what happens in life, we are always able to come back to a place of joy and fulfillment.

From this place, we are able to experience life with awe, wonder, curiosity, a sense of learning, and the playfulness of youth.

~ **Moneeka Sawyer**

Chapter One
My Journey to Bliss

There is something wrong with me.

I found myself thinking that every day.

No one had to tell me. It was something I knew deep down in my bones.

My mother and father came from Pune, India, to live in America—in a white, middle-class, suburban neighborhood in Columbus, Ohio. I was born here, but it was clear I wasn't *from* here. We not only looked different than everyone else, but everything about us was different—the food we ate, the clothes we wore, the way we talked, the holidays we celebrated.

I wasn't just different. I was wrong. Weird. Unacceptable.

I was the only nonwhite child in my elementary school, but even before my first day of school, I felt isolated and alone.

In kindergarten, Ellen and Alan were the only two classmates who would hang out with me. I don't know why they did when no one else would. Maybe it was because I always sat alone. Maybe it was because they were just two incredibly kind children with big hearts. Maybe it was because they felt different too.

On recess, we would go to a secluded spot on the playground away from the other kids. I didn't want to be around others. Out there, it wasn't safe.

One day, Ellen was sick and didn't come to school. Alan was called away and wasn't on recess. I was alone and on my own.

I looked around the playground and saw a group of six older girls playing jump rope near the tetherball court. I don't know what came over me, except that I was lonely for my friends and so wanted to be included.

I mustered up as much courage as I could and walked over to the six girls who were having so much fun. As I got closer, they stopped their game and stared at me.

"Can I jump rope with you?" I asked, trying to look and sound like someone they might accept.

They immediately burst out laughing.

Becky Peterson, a tall, lanky, gawky looking girl, was obviously the leader of this group. She looked me over from head to toe through her thick eyeglasses in utter contempt.

"We're not going to let Shit Face play, are we?" she asked the others haughtily.

I never asked to play jump rope again.

When I got home from dance class, Neelam, my little sister, was lying on her bed, crying into her pillow. I could tell she didn't want to be noticed, but I couldn't help myself.

"Neenum, what happened? Please tell me."

"They're so mean," she sobbed. "Why are they so mean?"

Even after leaving Ohio to live in San Jose, California, nothing seemed to have changed for us. I was no longer "Shit Face." Instead, I was "Miss Big Nose" or "Ape Arms." My little sister would never tell me what they called her. It was unspeakable, and I understood completely.

I tried to give her some comfort—it was my job as the big sister to protect her, but I couldn't even protect myself.

"Moneeka! Neelam! Dinner is on the table!"

We rushed to the kitchen, the smell of turmeric and cardamom filling my nostrils. Mom was an exceptional cook, and having dinner together was always the highlight of our day. At least at home, we were loved, accepted, and safe.

Now that I was in the third grade, it was my job to set the table. I put out the avocado-green plastic plates for the four of us and went to get the utensils and cups. Neelam, being two years younger, would handle the napkins.

"I know, I know," my mother said, consoling my father as she fussed over the pots on the stove.

He was clearly agitated.

"I mean, of course I didn't get it. I'm Indian."

Apparently, my father, a materials engineer, had once again been skipped over for promotion.

My mother, a doctor, was paid half what the other female doctors at the hospital earned—and who knew how much less than the male doctors. I can remember her saying, "They wouldn't treat me like this if I weren't Indian." It was often a topic of discussion at our house.

We were different. We didn't fit. We all knew it.

Mom filled our plates with rice and steaming *aloo gobi* as we settled in together around the dinner table.

"How was your day at school today, Moneeka?"

I looked at her blankly, the memories still playing out in my mind.

Today was PE. The kids always made fun of me. I was so tiny that I was always the last to be picked, and I was always teased. PE meant humiliation.

But today, we played dodgeball.

Dodgeball was where I excelled. I was so small and so quick that I was always the last one out. Today was no different.

Whoosh! The spongy red rubber balls came fast from every direction. All twenty kids surrounded me, trying to take me out. Whoosh! Another miss.

Suddenly, they began to chant in unison. "Get Big Nose! Get Big Nose!"

And in that moment, instead of aiming low for my body, the balls started coming at my head.

"Get her head! Get her head!"

It was like some maniacal cult of wicked children, all intent on causing me pain. I suddenly realized: They are actually trying to hurt me!

I ran frantically, trying to stay away from that ball, feeling trapped and scared, when our teacher Miss DeVries stormed into the group.

"What are you doing?" she asked with icy deliberation, her voice clipped and fierce.

The chanting stopped. Most of the kids looked down at the ground, scared and embarrassed. A couple snickered.

"PE is over," she stated firmly. "All of you sit on the bench until the bell rings. Then come into class single file."

She looked at me and said, "Follow me."

Miss DeVries led me into the quiet of our classroom, turned to me, and cradled my head in her hands, looking intently in my eyes. She was so kind. So tenderhearted. She would protect me.

"Are you okay?"

"Nobody here likes me," I replied.

She pulled me into her arms.

"I love you," she said.

"Moneeka," Mom repeated. "How was school today?"

"Fine," I whispered.

~~~~~

As I grew older, the bullying became more subtle and, in many ways, more painful. The jibes and jabs shifted from my physical differences to my identity, my character.

They stopped calling me Big Nose and Ape Arms. Instead, I was singled out for being a smart kid and for being nice. It was now "Geek" or "Dweeb." I was "Goody Two-Shoes" and "Teacher's Pet." It didn't matter how I looked—no one bothered to notice. Nobody even looked at me.

When a teacher would single me out for being intelligent, the insults would come at me from every side: "Smart Ass." "Show Off." "Egghead."

Loneliness followed me from junior high through high school. I had maybe two or three friends. More often than not, I felt as if I had none. Instead of having a social life, I devoted most of my time to my studies, to reading, and to dance. There, I was always safe from my loneliness and sadness.

In my sophomore year, though, everything changed. I got to go to Pune, India, to stay with my aunt and uncle, whom I affectionately called "Bhadi Ma" and "Cha Cha."

Back in India, I was no longer different and alone. Not only was I esteemed for being smart, in Pune, I was stared at for being so beautiful. *Me? Beautiful?!*

In the US, I was this hideous, ugly, deformed thing. In India, I was considered absolutely gorgeous. I was sixteen, and cute boys wanted to be around me. It was a culture shock of the best kind.

One day, Cha Cha took me to a street fair downtown. The sights and sounds filled me with happiness. I went from booth to booth, looking at all the amazing things to buy. People stared at me, and not just because I was singing "Born in the USA," with a full voice, as we shopped. For the first time in my life, I felt pretty, confident, and self-assured.

When I came to a booth filled with books in English rather than Hindi, I had to stop. I was a voracious reader. My eyes rested on a book with a compelling title: *Think and Grow Rich.*

I had decided I was going to be successful no matter what all those kids at home said about me, so this book immediately grabbed my attention. Next to it, I saw another book that intrigued me: Norman Vincent Peale's *The Power of Positive Thinking.* I quickly snatched that one, too.

And then, a bit farther away, I saw this striking book with an intense black cover. On it, there was a large picture of a typical Indian sculpture; it was a provocative image of a sensuous man intertwined with a voluptuous, beautiful woman. *The Secrets of Tantra,* was the title: *The Power of Using Your Sexual Energy for Attraction.* How could a sixteen-year-old girl resist?

Just as my hand reached out to touch that scintillating book, Cha Cha appeared.

"Ah, my dear, what did you find?"

I quickly showed him the Norman Vincent Peale.

"Oh, that is a great book! We shall read it together."

As he walked away, I picked up all three books, stuffed them under my jacket, and tossed more than enough money to the vendor, not caring about getting any change. I slowly walked away, following my uncle, as if nothing had happened.

I left *The Power of Positive Thinking* on the table next to my bed at home, but I hid the other two books under my mattress, along with a pen and the small notebook in which I would take copious notes.

After everyone was asleep, I'd turn on the little lamp near my bed and squint to read my secret treasures. These were books unlike the ones in America. The covers were smooth plastic, and the pages were thin as tissue. They were delicate, fragile things; I was always afraid that they would fall apart in my hands. When I opened them, they smelled of must and midnight, and sometimes the ink would stick the pages together and smudge, making the words hard to decipher.

I devoured all three books in a week, and then I reread them over and over again, taking more and more notes and becoming more and more entranced by what I was learning. Positive thinking. Growing rich. The power of attraction. I was transfixed, transformed.

All too soon, it was time to say goodbye to Cha Cha and Bhadi Ma. I returned to California to be with my parents and my two younger sisters. And I prepared once again to face the horror that was high school in America.

My trip to India and what I learned there didn't remove my fears of being an outsider at home in the United States. I went through my usual ritual of preparing for the trauma of returning to school: making my hair perfect, practicing my makeup for weeks, picking out the perfect outfit and laying it out three days before the first day of school.

I needed to put on my armor. I needed to protect myself from what was to come.

But this year, my junior year, I had one more weapon in my armory. From those magical books I found at the street fair, I had learned something about my mind and the power each one of us has. Our minds control *everything*. I was free to make decisions and to choose outside of what other people might think.

I had also learned that "normal" isn't all it's cracked up to be. In fact, I learned that if you aren't considered normal, that's something to celebrate: You're more likely to be successful in the end. Even me. Even Shit Face.

So on that first day back to my old high school, I made a conscious choice: I was going to smile the biggest smile and have a positive impact on every single person I met that day.

I cringe when I think of that first greeting I made. I put on the biggest, broadest smile, lit up my face in the most exaggerated way, and enthusiastically declared "Good morning!" to the first soul I encountered in the hallway. I'm sure I looked like a crazy woman. I must have scared her half to death.

"Oh!" she replied, in shock. "G-g-good morning!"

It was then that I realized the power of positive intentions. Even in my fear, there was power in embodying the positive. And I realized that, in being positive to everyone I met, I had so much more control over how people responded to me.

In fact, I didn't have a single negative experience all day.

When it came time for my Honors Algebra class, I almost lost my resolve. In this class were the two boys who had been the meanest and cruelest to me in the past. I remembered Dr. Peale's philosophy: *When you see someone, always send them a smile from your heart. You will affect their day just with that smile. And if it's someone you have problems with, smile even more.*

I walked into that classroom and sat right next to these two boys who had caused me so much pain. For the entire class, I sent them smiles and positive energy. Without saying a word, I sent them the best part of myself.

Just one week later, to my surprise and delight, we became study buddies.

I still had a lot to learn about positive intentions though—and about love. When I was attending U.C. Berkeley, I began dating Greg. I always knew he had a temper. He could get angry at the smallest thing.

But I loved him. I loved him madly. One day, I told myself, *I will marry him. Have babies with him. Raise a family with him.*

We were waiting in line at the theater for the latest blockbuster—a nice break from studying for midterms—when it happened. Some guy cut in line.

"Did you see that?" Greg was livid.

I took his hand in mine. "It's okay, sweetheart. Look! He's just joining his friends."

Greg didn't seem to care. He didn't find my reasoning helpful.

"He shouldn't do that. He needs to go to the back of the line."

"Sweetie. Can we just have a good time? Can we just forget about him and enjoy ourselves?"

I gave his hand a squeeze.

He squeezed back. Only he didn't stop squeezing.

He squeezed and he squeezed and he squeezed. Until finally, I heard and felt my hand crunch.

"Oh my God!" I started screaming. "What are you doing?"

My hand exploded in pain. It started to swell up. He didn't even look at it.

"We're outta here," he said.

I never thought Greg would hurt me intentionally, but, after that, I was hyper aware of his temper.

One night, we were planning to go out and meet friends for dinner. I asked Greg if he was ready to go, and he told me that he had a call to make for work before we left.

"Okay. Let me call Anne before you do that to let them know we'll be running a little late."

It seemed like a reasonable request. We only had one phone after all. But to Greg, it seemed like I was trying to control him. He told me, "No." He was firm and resolute.

"Honey, please. Can we at least call them first? It will only take a minute."

Anger. Harsh words. Sputtering.

In a moment, I felt myself crash into the wall. And after he shoved me, his arm flew up. He backhanded me in the face. I saw spots, splintered light, and knew for the first time, what getting a black eye felt like.

"I didn't mean it," he said, as I sobbed. "You just got in the way."

We never made it to dinner.

Still, I loved him. I loved him madly. But I also knew that I could never put myself in a relationship with a man where I felt like I was in danger. At one point, I made a choice.

I love this person so much, and I may never ever find someone I love as much as I love him again, but I can't live like this. I can't live with this. I'd rather be alone and safe than live in fear that I may be hurt again.

I said goodbye to Greg, and I said hello to myself.

Although I grew more cautious about the people I dated, I didn't exercise the same care with my platonic male friend Brian. We were both business majors at Berkeley, finishing up our senior year when he agreed to help me move into my new apartment.

After hauling boxes and furniture, I took him out for dinner to thank him for all his hard work. Brian asked me if I'd come back to his place and help him edit his paper. We did this a lot for each other, and since he had just helped me move, it seemed like it was the least I could do to show my appreciation.

He opened the door for me, and I walked in, tossing my bag on the sofa. When I heard the deadbolt click behind me, I turned to Brian, and he had this strange look on his face.

"What's going on?" I asked, confused.

Brian launched across the room and grabbed me.

Suddenly this 210-pound guy was on top of me on his bed. Pushing me down. It hurt!

"What the hell are you doing?" I screamed. "What is wrong with you?"

"What is wrong with me?" he growled. "You're what's wrong with me. You owe me."

He shoved his knee painfully between my legs. My skirt was ripped and hiked up my thighs. Fear surged through me.

"This is rape," I screamed.

"It's only rape if you don't want it. Stop struggling. Give it up."

I twisted and slammed my heel into his face. He yelped and lost his balance. I punched and kicked and screamed.

"You don't get to rape me, you asshole!"

I kicked hard again, and he tumbled to the side. I scrambled out from under him, ran across the room, struggled with the deadbolt, and was finally free in the fresh air. I sprinted to my car and locked myself in so he couldn't get at me again.

I couldn't believe that happened to me again. My senior year in high school, and now my senior year in college.

Both times, friends. Both times, guys I trusted.

I have no idea what came over him that night. I never saw it coming. I don't know why he tried to rape me.

I thought I was victorious. I didn't realize until later what had really happened to me.

Yes, I had baggage, but I didn't realize how much—not until I started having the dream.

I was lying in a coffin—not a softly padded, funeral home coffin, but the wooden kind vampires or mummies used in black-and-white horror films.

I had a pillow under my head, but my back was stiff against the hard, scratchy wood. I felt so cold.

Then the lid descended, the light around the edges becoming a sliver and then disappearing altogether. I was in total darkness, utterly alone.

Whoever had put me here was now nailing me in. I could hear the thud of the hammers against the nails and then against the wood of the coffin. I was trapped. Suffocating in fear. There was nothing I could do but scream.

I would beat against the lid of that wooden coffin and scream.

For two years, I would wake up screaming in the middle of the night.

For eight more years after that, I dreaded falling asleep. The nightmares were no longer every night—sometimes I'd go a week, sometimes I'd go a month or two. But that only made it worse: I never knew when the nightmare would return.

By then, David and I had married, and I had started my mortgage business six years before. It gave me the income I wanted but not the freedom. I was regularly working eighty-hour weeks. I was exhausted. Everything else in my life was dying. I couldn't sustain it any longer. I knew it. David knew it.

"I can't do this anymore," I told him.

He nodded his support. "I know. So what do we need to do about it?"

What we did about it was hire a coach for me.

Tyler was an amazing resource. Every week, we'd meet and dive deeply into the choices I was making and how I was relating to my life and my business. For three months, I began to see the ways I was sabotaging myself and my happiness. I took ownership. I made changes.

Then, it happened. All hell broke loose.

And that hell was me.

"What aren't you telling me?" Tyler asked.

There was only one thing I could think of. But every time it came to mind, I pushed it aside. I didn't see how it mattered. I didn't see what difference it made.

"I don't think it's pertinent."

"Let me be the judge of that. We seem stuck. What aren't you telling me?"

So I said to myself, *"What the hell?"* And then I told him about the attempted rapes.

Tyler looked at me and said, "You realize that you're responsible, don't you?"

WHAT?!

I cannot express the torrent of words that came out of my mouth. The screaming. The expletives. The verbal assault.

Tyler took it all. Not just then, but for the next week. Every day he'd call me. And every day he'd provoke me: "Why aren't you taking responsibility?" "When are you going to accept the part you played in this?"

For the first four days, all I could do was scream at him. On day five, I finally heard the truth:

"Moneeka, I'm not telling you that you're bad or that you deserved this happening to you. I'm telling you that you have to take responsibility for how you are dealing with these events in your life. You need to take responsibility for the fact that you don't trust people."

15

"You believe that you are always going to be betrayed."

Once those words landed, I stopped screaming. I began to sob. My body heaved with the emotion of it, and I fell out of my chair onto the floor.

Tyler was right. I was responsible. Not for the attacks, but for how I was relating to them.

"Until you take responsibility for the way you react to people doing things that hurt you, this will be a regular pattern in your life."

Tyler let me scream and cry. He listened. Most of all, he helped me see the reality that I was creating.

That night, my nightmares stopped. They have never returned. That was when I stepped onto the path that I now define as bliss. Along the way, I learned that, no matter what happens to us, the way we react to the events in our lives is what determines how we feel. And how we feel is more important than anything. That is what determines if we are happy or not. The events themselves don't do that.

I made a decision to be free, happy, and alive. Since that day of my decision, I have perfected the tools and skills that allow me to live that way. Through this journey, I have learned a lot about me and how to be a better me. I've stuck to my own dreams and not given up on myself regardless of the criticism I may receive. I finally have the strength to be able to renegotiate my relationships to make them more joyful for everyone involved. I started a whole new career that is more aligned with my values and desires. I've created an emotional foundation of strength and stability. Most important, I've truly created a life that I love.

Because of the joy I have discovered in my own life, I feel called to help others to achieve true bliss and contentment in theirs. I have the tools you can use to create your own blissful life, and I want to share them. So in this next phase of my life, I am inspired to teach and mentor others like you to move through your pain and learn how to live a life of boldness, happiness, and peace. As a part of that commitment, I have written this book.

This world is an amazing place, full of love and joy. It's also full of so many opportunities for growth. If we can all help each other experience more of the joy and love, the world will become a better and better place. I want you to experience that.

I hope, in the pages that follow, you will discover your bliss, choose it, and embody it in such a way that you help others finds and live their bliss, too.

Now, it's your turn to choose. Choose bliss.

Chapter Two
Core Values

"It's not hard to make decisions when you know what your values are."

~ Roy Disney

In any discussion of bliss, the very first thing we need to address is the topic of values. If we are not aligned with our own personal values in everything we do, it is impossible to feel true enduring bliss because there is always a part of us that is in conflict. This conflict creates disharmony inside of us and won't let us settle into a feeling of contentment and joy. Is your life aligned with your values?

The big obstacle to answering this question is that most people don't even know what their core values are. As a first step we should spend some time discovering and examining our core values.

Have you ever been in a situation where you should be happy? You were making good money. You were doing what you thought you are supposed to be doing, yet you were not fulfilled and, at best, you were just going through the motions. I've been there, and maybe you have too.

Sometimes, we experience a great deal of internal conflict between what we think we should be doing, what other people expect us to be doing, and what our core values are. If you don't do things according to your core values, you will without a shadow of a doubt experience regret, unhappiness, and lack of fulfillment in your life. That's because your core values really determine what is most important to you and what is going to make you feel the most joyful in everything that you do. Whenever you deviate from them you are going to experience problems.

Buddha wrote: "It is better to conquer yourself than to win a thousand battles. Then the victory is yours." Before that victory will come a struggle. Sometimes unexpected things happen in life. Maybe you need to align with the values of your family or of someone who needs your help at the moment. In the beginning you may think that you have to deviate from your values, but you should try to stay as aligned as you can with your own values. Those deviations stop happening once you are fully aligned with your values. At that point, you will be able to find ways to meet the needs of others while remaining true to yourself. Like everything else connected to your own personal growth, it is a process.

Let's think about a core value for a moment. If you say, "My core value is freedom," what does that mean? If what freedom means is that you don't want to be bossed about by somebody else, you really need to delve a little deeper. Do you want to have more autonomy in your job or do you want to have your own business? Let's say you decide to start your own business, but then after a time, you say to yourself, "I am aligned with freedom, but why I am still not happy?"

Any ideas? Well, maybe what freedom really means to you is the freedom to spend time with your family, and now that you have started this business that steals even more of your time, you see even less of them.

Think about how that plays out. Your business may now own you. You have less freedom according to your definition of it. You have less freedom than when you were employed in the dreaded day job. You have to realign your life with your core values. Here's how.

Start by defining what freedom really means to you. In this

case your real core value is having the flexibility to spend time with family. If that's the case, maybe you want to work part-time. Maybe you want to step down and take a job with fewer responsibilities instead of deciding to be an entrepreneur, which is probably the most time-consuming career in the world.

Now that freedom has a more accurate definition in your own internal value map you will be better able to make decisions to satisfy that value.

Great job—for someone else

A woman I know is a very successful life coach specializing in top fifty businesses, corporations, and leaders. Prior to that, she was in a job successfully selling second mortgages. However, that went against her core value of helping people. Everything was booming while she was talking people into taking money out of their home equity and acquiring more debt.

She said, "This doesn't align with my core values." Not surprisingly, even though she was successful, she wasn't happy. She also felt trapped in her job because she had to financially support her husband. Eventually she got divorced. After the divorce she said, "I don't have to support my husband anymore. I think I will do something that really matters to me." She decided to pursue a career as a life coach and hasn't ever looked back.

That's a good example of a mortgage broker whose core values were more about helping people than about making a lot of money. She started small, but because she's doing something that aligns with her core values her business has grown quickly. She now has a career where she gets to both help people and make a lot of money.

An Indian friend of mine took his culture's value of climbing to the top in any venture he engaged in seriously. He believed that if you are not moving up, something is wrong with you. His Indian wife carried the same belief. How do you suppose that translated into their careers? If you are working for somebody, you believe you must climb the corporate ladder. My friend started off as an intern in a company. He was then offered an engineering position, which he took. True to his beliefs, he climbed from Engineer up to scientist 1, 2, 3, and then he moved into management because he believed he needed to manage larger and larger teams and climb as high as possible.

As he moved up, he was getting both cultural pressure and pressure from his wife to continue advancing. One day as we had lunch, I pointed out that the really happy, smiley person I used to know had been replaced by someone somber and serious. Our conversation was not very energetic. "What's going on?" I asked.

He told me his passion was to create software. He really wanted to just be a programmer. So he wasn't aligned with this whole climbing the corporate ladder idea, even though he believed that he needed to do that. His core value was to be creative in his job and to create. As an engineer, he got to create products and then make them take shape. That filled him up. He was also learning, which was another core value for him. But now, in management, it was all about paperwork, meetings, and managing people. As much as he enjoyed the people part of it, leading people wasn't in his core values and his creative and learning engineering values were being neglected.

Ultimately, he moved back to technical work with another company where he could be more consistent with his core values. The new company's technical track was more robust, and he was able to grow his engineering and creative side. Finally, he could move up the corporate ladder in a way that allowed him to create, learn, and expand.

When I talked to his wife, she admitted that, yes, in the other job he had become kind of a grumpy guy to live with. When he decided to make the change, she was annoyed at first. Friends and family didn't understand. His decision meant that they were going to have to take a pay cut, but she supported him in that. She tells me now that it was worth it because living with him is much more pleasant than it was when he was in that funk. Once more, her husband comes home happy with many exciting stories about what he did during the day.

It pleases me that life has become more enjoyable for both of them. They are happier and still able to reach their personal, professional, and financial goals, all because he paid attention to his values.

Is your business a value-based one?

You need to be sure that your values align with the focus of your business. I used to be an executive coach. I dealt a lot with CEOs and I developed a deep understanding of why they couldn't expand their businesses. We explored many of the topics I address in this book about what they were looking for in their own lives and why they were not getting them. What had they given up for their business that might be causing disharmony with their personal value system? That eventually affected their performance.

Many psychological blocks can prevent us from performing effectively in life and business, and those issues were what I worked on with clients. We looked at their strengths and weaknesses, and we looked at their values. I'm proud that many of those executives were able to break through their barriers and come out stronger and more powerful than before. I have also worked with a lot of self-employed people. My goal with all of them was to help them live according to their values.

A really key piece to that is running a value-based business. Closely related to that is what I call passion management rather than time management. Where are you spending your time? Is it with the things that you are passionate about and really align with your values including your spiritual values? When you go out into the world, running your business, are you acting with passion and your core values or are you basing your actions on what other people tell you?

Values and relationships

You need to pay attention to your own values in your personal life as well. For instance, suppose you meet somebody and they seem really fascinating, like the kind of person you want to hang out with. However, as you get to know them, you realize they don't align with your core values. Perhaps you continue that friendship or relationship in spite of that for whatever reason, but you will find that you are never going to be deeply happy in this relationship unless it aligns with your values. It doesn't mean that you have to have the exact same values. It just means that your values need to be close enough so that the relationship is aligned with your own values.

My husband and I went through an exercise of values together. I have to say that I was really pleased to find that we had completely aligned values for the most part. All of our top values are the same, but they show up in a different order. For instance, my very top value is relationships/family. His very top value is learning, while learning is number five for me. Family is number three for him. So initially, when we started our relationship, there was conflict because he wanted to spend all of his time at work, and I felt like a newlywed widow. However, once we actually had a conversation about what he needed and what I needed, it became completely different. We were able to negotiate and adjust so he was not always at work. Two nights a week when he worked late, I decided to attend dance practice. That wasn't just a case of my trying to occupy the time he was gone. Having time to be creative and dance was one of my core values as well.

Instead of our relationship being all about my husband's desire to go work and learn, leaving me feeling deserted, we have negotiated a schedule that really works for both of us and fills both of our needs, according to our values.

Once you are aware of your values, you have something solid that you are willing to stand up for and negotiate around rather than just arguing, blaming, or pointing fingers. Now you can say,

"Let's align our values because that's important."

When core values conflict

There are times when your own personal core values seem to conflict with each other. Part of what I teach in my workshops is what to do when you have conflicting or seemingly conflicting values. How do you bring them into alignment with one another? How do you deal with them when they come up in life? It takes a little finessing.

Here's an example. Regardless of your culture, your values are still your values. In my Indian culture, weddings and funerals are the things that family and friends would never think of missing. Of course, sometimes you have to miss them, but for me, that's a very high priority. This isn't just a cultural obligation for me. Over the years, I have found that this is something that I really want to commit to because it aligns with my values. Because I am the oldest cousin in our entire family, I am kind of like the big sister. I want to be there. It is an honor that my family members feel that way about me.

Unfortunately, I have missed a couple of weddings when I was younger because of extenuating circumstances, but in my view, going to a wedding is a non-negotiable. However, I was recently asked to speak at a three-day workshop in Sacramento. I was thrilled at the prospect and knew it would help my business tremendously. I would be speaking on the second day of the event, so people could get to know me and warm up to me at the beginning, and then we would have another day and a half for them to connect with me after my speaking piece. Two days after I made the commitment to this, I got a Save the Date from one of my cousins who was getting married.

I was in a quandary. I kept thinking, "What am I going to do? I can't miss a wedding, and I can't miss this opportunity for my career either."

The decision I made was based on my core values. It wasn't a reactive one making this an either-or situation. I couldn't do both, so I knew I needed to renegotiate the speaking engagement. Integrity is also important to me and I had given my word, so I didn't want to cancel on the producer of the event. Fortunately, the speaking engagement was four months away. Were I to bow out, the facilitator had time to find another speaker. But he said he really wanted me there because what I talk about is very aligned with what he wanted his people to experience. What we did was change when I spoke. My conflict was solved that easily.

Instead of speaking on the second day, I spoke on the first day. I had less time to meet with people, but I got to go to the wedding, which was very important to me.

Had I not been aware of my core values I could very easily have said, "This is an important opportunity. I am trying to grow a business, and I need to make this a priority." Had I done that, I would have felt horrible and regretted it for a long time.

I would have been miserable at either one of those events had I taken another path and backed out of either one of them. Being so fully aware of my values and my priorities enabled me to make clear decisions and have clear negotiations around those decisions.

That's another benefit of knowing your values. You can make your decisions, not from emotion, not from feelings like guilt or greed that might be trying to direct that decision. Instead, you can make your decisions based on your core values. Believe me, tough decisions are easier to make when you are clear on those values.

I told this story during the speech at that conference because I wanted people to understand why I was leaving early and why values are important. It gave me more credibility to demonstrate that I was living by my values.

It's interesting to note that people around you realize when you are living by your values. They also notice if you are living through reaction. Most people only see the way that you live. They don't usually sit down with you to talk about your values. But they get to know what yours are through your actions. My family knows that if there is a wedding, a funeral, or other big event, something that's very important to them, I will bend myself into a pretzel to be there because they matter that much to me. If it turns out that I can't be there, there is no explanation ever required because they know that I am true to my values. My family members know who I am, no explanation required.

Even if the person you love doesn't have your same values, you can still align with that and say, "I really get that, and I really want to support you in that, but I need a little bit more support in our relationship. What can we do?" Allow the other person to come up with solutions that will work for them, so you can work through it together. Try whatever solution you come up with, and if it doesn't work, try another solution until you come up with something that's really going to work and flow in your life. In a few more years, you may need to renegotiate it. Being clear on what your core values are is a relationship builder with yourself. It's also a relationship builder with the people you care about. If you want to love somebody, if you want to have that person in your life, you have to accept that you can't change them. You have to align with them. But it doesn't mean that you have to give up your own values in favor of theirs.

Deal breakers

Maybe you value having a big family, and the person you are dating does not want children. That's going to be a value conflict that's probably unresolvable. There are definitely values that are not compatible. If one partner values honesty, and the other one speaks out of both sides of their mouth, you are going to have a value conflict. That relationship is probably not going to work.

Isn't it wonderful to find that out in the beginning of a relationship rather than bang your head against the wall wondering why your relationship isn't working? It would be better to stop fooling yourself that maybe someday he is going to want kids, or that maybe someday she is not going to want to steal from everybody she works with. If your values conflict you can actually leave the relationship on good terms. You don't make each other wrong or bad. You can simply agree that you have different values and aren't a good long-term match.

Chapter Three
Beliefs and Limitations

"Stop acting small. You are the Universe in ecstatic motion."

~ **Rumi**

You just learned the importance of core values. Let's look at our default ways of thinking. That is, those beliefs and thoughts that go through our minds that we can group into buckets.

Judgmental thinking

The first bucket of thought is being judgmental. We overgeneralize and jump to conclusions based on a past event or piece of evidence. We judge others based on a belief system that doesn't have any real consistent support for it.

Many people from India, myself included, live in the Silicon Valley of California. A lot of them have come in with H1B visas and get hired as engineers. Many people in our area make statements like this: "These Indians are just coming to this country, taking our jobs, and they are sending the money back to India. The money isn't even circulating here." That's being really judgmental about a particular group of people in the community. Yet Indians are huge consumers. Anybody who thinks that the money isn't coming back into the community doesn't know us. Although some do send money back home, oh my goodness, we spend so much money right here! The statement is judgmental, a generalization, and not even true.

That is just one overgeneralization about a community conflict. I think all of us are judgmental. I remember watching *Avenue Q*, a Broadway musical. One of the songs, "Everyone is Racist," addresses the fact that all of us have our judgmental sides. They talk about racism in particular, but there are many ways in which we can be judgmental. When we make blonde jokes, Jewish jokes, poor people jokes, rich people jokes, or crazy cat-lady jokes, we are being judgmental. The word *prejudice* really means *pre-judge* and a lot of the time we don't have real foundation for those judgments.

I like to make a distinction between judgment and discernment. For me, judgment is an opinion that's not well-founded but that we stick to. It's often an overgeneralization of a group of people or a type of person. A discernment is based on something we have learned or experienced. Maybe I have discovered that when I have this kind of interaction, I am not going to get along well with that person, and maybe that's not the kind of person I want to have in my life. Or that's not the kind of job I want to have in my life, or that's not the kind of person I want to work with. That discernment is simply based on experience and wisdom.

We don't have to like everybody, be friends with everybody, and work with everybody. We do need discernment about who we are going to have in our life, but that's a very different thing than being judgmental.

Black-and-white thinking

This occurs when people think all events, things, people, and decisions are black and white or good or bad, and there is no gray area.

All cat ladies are crazy. Is that really true? Maybe one woman has a really, really big heart and she saved a whole litter of kittens. All blondes are stupid. Maybe you just bought into the stereotype of blondes portrayed in early Hollywood myths.

Topics like politics, school prayer, and saluting the flag all fall into this category. If you think those issues are black and white then you leave no room for exploration of what's really going on. It is a form of judgmental thinking.

Judgment doesn't make you actually think about the issue, event, or people. This type of thinking keeps you trapped in your own mind and in your judgment, and it doesn't allow you to expand and really connect with people. It prevents you from learning and keeps you really stuck.

Mindreading

Mindreading is when we assume that we know what people are thinking or why they are doing something. We assume that they think and feel exactly the way we do, and that's just not true. We assume that they have the same thought process, same knowledge, same experiences, and same beliefs as we do, and therefore, they should be thinking a certain way or feeling a certain way.

This doesn't leave room for other people to be different from us. A friend of mine and her boyfriend were celebrating her birthday and he gave her a really funny card with a Jamba Juice gift card.

She leapt to the conclusion that "Obviously, he doesn't love me much."

It's true the card wasn't sentimental. It didn't have lots of flowery poetry about how beautiful she was and how much he loved her. And, no, he didn't get her jewelry or something more personal. It was a card that was supposed to make her laugh, and it contained something that she could use to buy something he knew she liked.

"I feel like you are trying to read his mind," I told her, "and what you are doing is projecting what's in your mind into his mind instead of really paying attention to what he personally was thinking."

"But it wasn't romantic at all," she insisted.

"It was romantic in his view. In his mind making you laugh and making you feel good are the ways that he expresses love for you. He knows you love Jamba Juice, so what better gift than to give you a ton of it? He can't do that, but he can give you a gift card."

Just because you think a certain way, doesn't mean that other people think that same way. When they do something differently, you can't assume that you can read their minds and know what they are thinking. You just have to assume that they think differently. This leads back to being judgmental. You are basically judging people for being different than you are.

Another version of mindreading is projection. You put yourself in another person's place and assign your motives to him or her. I have a friend whose sister journals all the time.

"I am concerned about Jane," my friend said.

"Why?" I asked. "She seems fine."

"No, she's always journaling now. She obviously must be in a lot of pain."

"You have to be in pain to write in a journal?" I asked.

"Well, it's the only time I journal," she said. "Just when I am in pain and really need to work through some stuff."

"Great," I told her. "That's a good tool for you, but it is a tool that people use in a variety of different ways in their lives, and it is not just to work through pain. I wouldn't be concerned about Jane. If you are interested, you might talk to her about what's going on in her life, but I wouldn't automatically assume that she is in pain because she's journaling."

So again, we have an individual who is mindreading. And judging. As it turned out—and as you probably guessed—Jane was just fine. It was my friend who had a mindreading and projection problem.

Dramatizing

Let's start by admitting that dramatizing just makes life so much more interesting, and it is a really natural place for us humans to go. As storytellers, which we have been since the tribe emerged, we are taught to dramatize. If you overdramatize in a negative way, such as expecting the worst in life when something goes wrong, you will make it more dramatic than it is by attributing feelings that don't actually exist. People who dramatize often start to worry about what's the worst thing that could happen. They worry about it, talk about it, feel the fear of it. As they do this, they emphasize the negative and trivialize the positive.

I mentioned my friend who was mindreading based on her boyfriend's choice of birthday gifts. Dramatizing would be taking that assumption to the next level. Waiting for the breakup, for instance. Imagining the breakup. Having a tantrum and creating the breakup because then she would have a big story to tell everyone. *He did this to me, and then, because I felt I had a right to tell him what I really thought, I said that. And then, he said this. And then, we got into this big fight. Then he, of course, stomped out, and I texted him and said, "I don't want to have anything to do with you, and I am breaking up."*

How the heck did that happen when he was trying to express love for you? Couldn't she have just had a conversation instead of assuming, dramatizing, and expecting the worst?

Comparing ourselves to others

This is being really self-centered. We have a propensity to think that people are actually paying attention to what we are doing, and that what they are doing is in relationship to us. We imagine that they are always thinking about us, and therefore, planning, plotting, and reacting to us personally. We compare ourselves to others and assume that they are doing the same to us.

For instance, if you are giving a talk, and somebody leaves, you assume it's that they didn't like what you were saying. But maybe they have another appointment scheduled. They might need to make a phone call. Maybe they just have to use the bathroom. They could leave your talk for any number of reasons. Yet the first thought you have before you rationalize it is: *Oh, I wonder if I offended them, or they must not think I am interesting, wonderful, and fabulous.*

I absolutely adore my in-laws, but culturally we come from very different worlds. I am first-generation Indian, and I was brought up in a very sheltered Indian home. My in-laws are third-generation Californians. As you can imagine, we have a lot of interactions that none of us always understand. I might go out to dinner with my husband and his parents and say something that's very, very natural for an Indian to say, something that just rolls off my tongue. But no one reacts the way that I expect, the conversation moves to another subject, and there is no closure.

When we get home, my first question to my husband is, "Do you think they are upset with me?"

"What are you talking about?" he says. "They love you," which I know is true.

"But the whole table went quiet," I tell him, "and then they just changed the subject. Maybe they are mad at me."

"They probably just didn't know what to say to that, and they moved on," he might say. "I am sure they don't even remember that piece of the conversation."

I learned that I might get all caught up in their reactions about what I said and what I did, when the topic wasn't even part of their world anymore.

We assume that people are paying a lot of attention to us, what we are saying, and what we look like, and we feel judged. We feel like people are reacting to us when that isn't the case. Why?

Because most people are just like you are. They are thinking about themselves. When we think everybody else is thinking about us, it can create heartache and misunderstanding. This in turn creates unnecessary drama.

Would have, should have, could have

We—you and I—have a list of beliefs about how we and other people should act in any given situation. If they break the rules, we get angry. If we break the rules, we may feel guilt, shame, and anger toward ourselves. We judge what we or someone else should have done, could have done, or would have done if they were good people, or if they really understood the situation. This is the root of a lot of our guilt in regard to relationships. How many times have you thought: *That person was really hurting. I should have said something nicer? I should have said something more supportive.* Or: *That person had a milestone birthday. I should have sent flowers. I could have called.* That, of course translates to: *This was my milestone birthday, and they didn't show up to my party. They at least could have called. I would have called.*

There are all these things that we should have done, could have done, or would have done, but really all those things are fantasy. They are tied into our judgments of people, into what's right and wrong, our black-and-white thinking, and they don't serve us in any way. All they do is make us feel bad, make us feel regret, and make us feel guilt and shame. They cause distance between people because they create unrealized expectations.

In the same way you mentally beat yourself up, you mentally beat other people up and create separation in relationships. For instance, with my girlfriend whose boyfriend gave her the funny card. "He should have known what I wanted," she told me. "I wouldn't have been so thoughtless."

We need to forget the *should have, would have, could have* and just accept what *is* and how people *are*. When you have a reaction, learn from it. Take that wisdom, and do better next time. Don't beat yourself up or create distance in your relationships. That is not going to benefit you.

The need to be right

If you constantly try to validate your own opinions and beliefs, you will go to great lengths to prove you're right. When you think people are judging you as wrong, it can create great pain and anger. All of us fall into this, at least some of the time, where we really want validation. We want to feel special. We want people to recognize us. Because of that, we might stand our ground on an issue, even after someone has proven us wrong.

We find this a lot of times with people we love. Maybe your spouse says, "I will meet you at five o'clock for dinner," and you are shopping, and you don't get there until 5:30. You could come up with all kinds of reasons to justify why you are late when, really, you should just apologize. However, if your need is to be right, you are not going to admit that you got distracted and forgot about the time.

On the job, a lot of people think the only way they can stay employed is to be right. They feel threatened if someone tells them they may be wrong. You also see it in the classroom. For instance, maybe a professor has a certain way of teaching, and then somebody in the class questions him. The professor refuses to hear it because he needs to be right.

The problem is that when you get stuck in your need to be right you restrict yourself from learning and expanding. You also offend other people and repel them. It has the opposite effect than what you were hoping for. Instead of getting more respect from others, you get less.

He did, she did

This is about scorekeeping and point-taking, which we do both with individuals and organizations. We expect them to notice what we have given, sacrificed, or done for them, and we expect them to reciprocate to the same degree. Furthermore, we feel bitter when the rewards we get for our own actions are not what we expected. We carry the belief that all rewards and recognition of our efforts should be noticeable and from the same person or organization that we did something for.

Let's compare this to the new thought of paying-it-forward. This concept tells us that if someone did something nice for me, I should do something nice for someone else. It could be anybody else. This goes against our natural inclination to reciprocate in kind to the specific person or organization that did something for us.

For example, if you invited me to your party, I am going to invite you to mine. If you picked up the tab at dinner last time, I am going to pick up the tab tonight. Life isn't always that simple though.

When I got out of U.C. Berkeley and landed my first job in a corporation as a receptionist, the CEO of the company had an affinity for me. Here I was, with a college degree working for a temp agency as a receptionist. It was the right company—just not the right position, the right work, or the right pay.

When I left college, I had big dreams: A high-paying corporate job, work that I loved in marketing, a fast-track to the C-suite. Things weren't turning out as I'd hoped.

After a few months, a co-worker stopped by the reception desk with a message: "Amal wants to see you in her office."

I immediately went to her office and tapped on the open door.

"Moneeka, please sit down," she said.

I sat.

"I hear that you are looking for other positions; that you want to leave us."

Amal was the CEO. She always smiled and said hello to me every morning. She knew my name, but I assumed that's all she knew. How did she know I was looking for work? More important, why did she care?

"I went to school at Berkeley," I explained. "I have a business degree in marketing. Working for a temp agency being a receptionist was never my goal. I need to find a position in marketing to use my degree and my talents."

Amal said she understood. She said it made perfect sense, and then she said, "I'm sorry, but we don't have any openings in marketing right now."

"Right," I said. "I know. And that's why I am looking for a position elsewhere."

She paused. And then she sighed. "You are so bright," she said. "You have so much potential."

"Thank you," I said, and I got up to leave.

"Give me two weeks."

Two weeks later, Amal had created not only a position but an entire department for me. I was so honored. It was so perfect. The only way I could ever repay this CEO was to work really hard at my position so that her company would succeed. There wasn't anything that I could really do for her personally. No amount of "thank you's," flowers, or cards was going to hold a candle to the gratitude that I felt for her belief in me. But what could I do? I repaid her by being a mentor to someone else. Like she did for me, I recognized someone else for their potential and helped lift them up. Instead of paying back that CEO directly, I paid it forward.

Chapter Four
Ego is Your Friend

"The Ego is an exquisite instrument. Enjoy it, use it—just don't get lost in it."

~ **Ram Dass**

Every time I address ego in a talk, I get lots of questions. The first one is how do I define the ego. Well, your ego is your conscious mind, the part of your identity that you consider your *self*. I think the ego gets a really bad rap. It is so often confused with egomania, vanity, or self-centeredness and other kinds of nasty things. But strictly speaking, it is only a psychological term popularized by Freud meaning the conscious as opposed to the unconscious mind or the awareness of one's own identity and existence. It is the part of you that defines itself as personality.

In many spiritual communities today, the focus is on the idea that the ego considers you, your person, a separate entity from the rest of the universe. Your ego differentiates you from the universe rather than making you one with it. Perhaps it was necessary for survival in some bygone days, but in modern times, it leads only to separation and delusion. This is why I think so many people talk about the ego as being the enemy, about how it causes separation and a delusional view of the world. Because of modern-day teachings, many of us have come to believe that this is true. But I'd like to remind you that your ego is a part of you. How does it feel to be in battle against a part of yourself? Trying to ignore it, get rid of it, or defeat it isn't possible. It's important to remember that bliss and battle can't take place in the same space.

No part of you is an enemy. All parts of us make up the whole wonderful being that we are, and we can't reject one piece and say that it is bad. Loving ourselves is about loving all of ourselves, every single piece, and bringing all of those pieces into balance. The reality is that the ego (as long as it's healthy) is a necessary part of us, without which we wouldn't be able to interact in society. It helps us to function in the world. It is a filter for both what we express from within us as well as what is allowed into us, and it has a lot of control over that flow. You need to make it your friend and in sync with the rest of you, which is all those other parts that need to have a voice. These other pieces include your spiritual self, heart self, child self, intellectual self, and others. As you spend time looking at your internal makeup, you will get to know all the parts of yourself. They are different for each of us. Your ego needs to be in sync with you so that it uses those filters to support all parts of you in the best way possible. A healthy, balanced ego is actually the key to attaining bliss while functioning in the world.

An unbalanced ego feels the need to be in charge, desires approval, and thinks it knows everything. It is never satisfied, and believes it knows what is best for you. It maintains control by way of voices in your head. It can create feelings of defeat or negative beliefs.

An unbalanced ego might tell you things like:

- *I am not good enough.*
- *Nobody likes me.*
- *That was stupid of me.*
- *I am so much better than all those people.*

Or

- *I know he is kind of a jerk, but I will stay with him because he's the best I can do.*

- *Of course you lost the deal; you really are not good enough. Try harder.*
- *If you lost more weight, you would be more attractive.*
- *Don't dream so big. You are really not that deserving.*

When it is out of balance, ego gives you a false sense of who you are, either by creating an overly negative self-image (like *You need to get better*) or an overly positive one (like *You are better than everyone else*).

As long as you have relationships with people, a healthy ego must exist. It understands the rules of human interaction and finesses the way we present ourselves in situations with other people. If you were completely ruled by your child self, without the filters of the ego, you might throw a tantrum every single time you didn't get something you wanted. If you completely suppress the ego and tried to live as your complete spiritual self, if you go to work, sit down, chant *om*, or work at your own pace, you would not be taking into consideration the goals of your employer or those around you. You would probably get fired. These are examples of how the ego helps us filter what we put out to the world. It also filters what we take in from the world.

Every moment we are exposed to thousands of different stimuli. If we had no filters our senses would go into overload. Together our brain and our ego filter out a lot. Without the filters of the ego, we would take personally everything that people say to us, or do around us. We would go into overload. The filter of the ego manages our perception of the outside world so we have the freedom to look at all the other pieces inside ourselves. When you are not overloaded with constant stimuli, you have the energy to pay attention to what is going on inside of you. You are not constantly focused outward. If spirituality is all about self-discovery, introspection, and connecting with the divine, then the ego is, in fact, your real-world spiritual solution. The ego is one of your selves. It can be a productive team-member with all the other parts of you, just make sure that it isn't the primary focus of everything you do. You don't want the ego to be your team captain.

The ego really helps us to function effectively in society. It must be accepted, nurtured, and taken care of. We shouldn't always be arguing with it. If you are, it's time to make peace with it. Fighting it or ignoring it doesn't make it go away, it only causes unnecessary internal struggle.

How ego looks when it's driving you:

- Impress the World – will do anything to get acceptance.
- Tear you down – unfair comparisons to others.
- Drive you to do things that will make you appear one way on the outside, which won't help you on the inside.

Let's define the other side of the ego that is ignored by most of the popular teachers out there today. Let's look at the EGO as **Energy-Giving Options.** An ego that is in balance helps to drive you and motivate you to succeed. It puts words to the dreams you have deep inside, and it grounds those dreams. Ego gives your voice, dreams, and ideas verbal and visual representation in the world. You could say it is like the cover on a really good book! It is the thing that draws people to the good, juicy stuff inside.

But the truth is, the cover doesn't mean anything if the book is a mess on the inside. It might draw people in, but it can't stand alone. Think of all the parts of you as a Mastermind Group.

Whenever a problem comes up, the ego is the first to jump in and start talking.

For example: You get a new job, and you need to find a new house.

Ego says: *Let's move into that neighborhood. It looks nice and will impress all your friends.*

Your heart self: *But I want a house that is easy to clean and more aligned with our finances.*

41

Ego: *Well, yes, but you should want a bigger house. You always go for smaller houses.*

Heart Self: *But that will cause me all kinds of financial and emotional stress.*

Ego: *Can we at least find something in a nice neighborhood?*

Heart Self: *I really like that idea, so of course.*

Ego: *Thank you. We will find something we can afford.*

Giving your ego a voice allows you to negotiate with it so all parts of you can be heard and honored.

Your ego will always be a rider on your bus of life. Accept it. Give it a seat, buckle it in, and be prepared to let it have a permanent place. What's driving your decisions? What motivates your decisions? What filters do you put those decisions through? What criteria do you use to make your decisions? Your job is to be aware of when your ego is taking over in an unhealthy way and then move it to the support stage from the fight state.

Question your reactions. Remember to give others the benefit of the doubt. Let's say you come home, and the dishwasher is still full. Ego jumps in with *OMG! Seriously? How many times do I need to tell him to unload the dishwasher?*

What if, instead, you took a deep breath, thought about it for a moment, and realized that your sweetie has been home late every night because he's been swamped at work and just couldn't get to the dishwasher and also give you some of his time? How different would the outcome be?

It begins with: Stop, Drop, and Breathe. Stop, and break the pattern you are in. Drop into your heart. Breathe at least 5 to 10 breaths. This gives you just enough time to interrupt the momentum of your ego taking over so you can become more aware and notice what is going on inside of you.

In order to bring the ego into balance, you have to actually start paying attention to it. Bringing it into balance will be hard at first. You may need to start over and over again. Over time, you will eventually find it is easy, but you need to start by taking baby steps.

"Success doesn't always make you happy, but happiness always makes you feel like a success."

~ Moneeka Sawyer

Chapter Five

What's (Self) Love Got to Do With It?

"Love is not something we give or get; it is something that we nurture and grow, a connection that can only be cultivated between two people when it exists within each one of them—we can only love others as much as we love ourselves."

~ **Brené Brown**
Research professor, University of
Houston Graduate College of Social Work

Brown's research really backs up a lot of the things that I have been talking about. I was recently listening to her tell a story about a time she was speaking to three thousand academics in Social Work in San Antonio, TX.

She asked the audience, "How many of you talk about love?"

Two hands went up.

Then she said, "Let me ask you this. How many of you today would be willing to walk outside of this room and never experience love again?"

No one raised their hand.

"How many of you believe that love is the absolute most important human experience?"

Everyone raised their hands.

"Then why aren't we talking about it?" she asked.

I agree with Brené Brown. My question is, why is it that most of us don't acknowledge love as one of the core tenets of living a life of bliss? Why don't we acknowledge what an important role it plays in our success in life?

We know that we want it. We know that we feel it. But to many of us, especially here in the United States, it is considered a "second-hand emotion," as singer Tina Turner would say. We may think of it as this thing that we do kicking and screaming against our will, and it tears us down and makes us weak. We have all these weird ideas of what love is, but the truth is that love is the *only* thing. Love is the only thing on this planet that none of us wants to live without. The first thing to really understand about love, loving yourself, and loving other people, is that we *need* love. Without it, we barely exist. This chapter is all about finding out how to make that love happen in the most beautiful, authentic way possible in your life.

True unconditional love starts with self-love. Unconditional love is complete acceptance, trust, and respect for who you are without judgment. Judgment can be defined as thoughts that are layered with opinions, beliefs, and values that are often created outside yourself and frequently not justifiable. Unconditional love requires no judgment, and I think that as human beings, because of who we are, we have a really hard time achieving that. We are all on the love spectrum. Some of us can't feel any love. Some are afraid to feel it. Others are so close to that ideal of unconditional love that they just glow and shine as an expression of love. For most of us, unconditional love is a pretty difficult thing to achieve. We need a base point of what it looks like, a reference point.

If you have children, you know that the moment that child is born, there is just this little bundle of new life that is lying there in your arms. All you feel is unconditional love. There is no expectation, no demand. There is no need. In that moment, everything else falls away, and all you are is connecting in love with this child. As that child grows up, you engage in fantasies about who that person is going to become. You have expectations and hopes and desires. You still love that child as a perfect being, and a parent loving a child is the very closest you can get to unconditional love. But those things that you attach to that child, those expectations, those desires, hopes, and dreams are still all projections of yourself, which means, in its truest form, that's not unconditional love because you are not fully accepting that being exactly as he or she is. I am not saying that that's wrong or bad by any stretch of the imagination. I am just trying to provide a little bit of clarity about how you might look at unconditional love.

The first step toward any relationship and to feeling love is, of course, to love yourself. This does not mean at all that it is about your ego. I am not saying to you that you should become a self-centered ego-maniac. When we are talking about unconditional love, we are not talking about ego-based love. As we've already discussed, your ego is a layer of protection or a mask or a façade that acts as a filter going in and out of your being for how you present into the world. What you have going on in the inside, you feed to the world through the ego, and the ego adjusts it in a way that it feels it will be acceptable to society. Then, the ego takes what it sees in society and feeds it back into us, which helps us to create a self-image and identify with what the world sees us as.

When you have a healthy ego you are less concerned with what the world is seeing and identifying you as and more in touch with who you identify yourself as. Then your ego plays more of a role in filtering *out* than filtering *in*.

Maybe you do believe you love yourself, but that love for yourself is wrapped in a layer of other ego-based emotions. For instance, if you have been hurt before by a man, the ego may say: *You should never be treated badly by a man.* Then you try to identify self-love and think: *I don't deserve to be treated that way, He is going to miss me. I did so much for him, and look at the way that he treated me.* You identify that as self-love, as if you are defending yourself as being a

47

really good, loving person. In this case, what's wrapped around your core of love is anger, bitterness, defensiveness, regret, resentment, sometimes guilt or shame. But I am not talking about an ego-based love, where there are all these other emotions wrapped around it. I'm talking about pure internal love. This pure love has no mask and nothing else packaging it. It is just the absolute core of love, and when you have it, you express love in a completely different way. When it comes out and it is filtered through your ego to the outside world, it is not wrapped up in anger, bitterness, and hurt. Instead, it is a true expression of who you are, and then the ego presents you as a shining light of love.

The deeper you tap into the core of unconditional love, the more you become unconditional love. So how do you tap into the beautiful core inside of you? Many teachers say the only real true way to access that internal love and acceptance for ourselves and true bliss is through meditation. Over the years, that belief has actually scared me because I am not a person who meditates. I have tried it. I often try to put it into my life, and I can do it for short periods of time if I am taking a personal development class or I am working through some issues. Even though I do meditation during those times, it is not something that ever sticks in my life.

It absolutely benefits me, and meditation is an amazing practice for becoming aware of what that core unconditional love is. Yet, as you will see in this book, I am not a person to ever advocate struggling against yourself to achieve bliss. I am really about fitting bliss in your life in a way that is aligned with who you are. If you have to work too hard for it, you are not going to continue in that direction. Since sitting in quiet meditation doesn't really work for me, I have found other ways to create that awareness inside of myself, and I have an awareness practice that does work. Every day when I am doing a task I need to do, I will give it more of my awareness. During that activity, I take deep breaths. I focus on the breath, slow things down, and focus internally. Anything that I am doing in that moment becomes a living, moving meditation. My favorite way to do this is to dance, and we will talk a little bit about movement in another chapter later on.

I am a dancer and so my deepest meditative moments happen when I am in movement. I have met many other people who become very meditative while they are cleaning, doing dishes, or even while they are getting ready in the morning, brushing their teeth, and washing their faces. Some people can do it in the shower. Wherever you are—even in the shower—deepen your breath, slow down, and just really be aware of your insides. That's what I do in order to get to this place of awareness where I can find that core of unconditional love.

Unconditional love just is. At your core, you are a being of unconditional love, but you need to tap into that. The living meditation I just described is one way, but there are other practices that can help you become more and more aware consciously of how you are loving yourself and how much more closely you are moving toward unconditional love. As you move closer to that place of unconditional love you will notice that your reactions in the world are going to be different.

The world is a mirror to who we are in any given moment, so when you move closer to that core, you are going to see that you are reacting differently in the world. When someone cuts you off in traffic, you are not going to fly into a rage. When your children don't get ready fast enough in the morning, you are not as likely to lose your patience. When your sweetie comes home and says something really, really irritating, you are more likely to be compassionate rather than blow up. When your boss hands you another task to do, you are less likely to become overwhelmed. You will start to see that this love inside of you starts to express itself outside of yourself. You can monitor your own progress that way.

There are conscious ways for us to get access to this. The first one is gratitude, which we'll discuss in depth later. Being grateful to yourself and for who you are is a huge part of loving yourself. Being grateful for what you bring to the world, being grateful for your gifts, being grateful for your capacity to take care of people like your children, being grateful for the talents that you bring to work.

The second one is self-awareness. This is being aware of your self-talk. Such as when you say anything like, "That was really stupid of me," or "I can't believe I just did that," or "Oh my god. I am such a ditz." Any of those statements are judgmental self-talk that say to your unconscious mind and to your inner being: *I don't love you. I am judging you.* Or: *I love you, but I don't love you unconditionally. And this is how I am judging you.* Anytime you start to see yourself doing that sort of thing, you must interrupt the thought. You can do this through self-inquiry. Ask yourself: *Wait a minute. Why I am treating myself that way? Why am I talking to myself that way?* If you can catch it, you can say something like: *Oh, that wasn't really stupid of me. I just made a mistake.*

A more structured method of this kind of self-inquiry has been taught by Byron Katie. It is known as *The Work of Byron Katie* or simply as *The Work*. While in a halfway house for women with eating disorders she experienced a life-changing realization. "I discovered that when I believed my thoughts, I suffered, but that when I didn't believe them, I didn't suffer, and that this is true for every human being. Freedom is as simple as that. I found that suffering is optional. I found a joy within me that has never disappeared, not for a single moment."

According to her, you just need to ask yourself, "Is that true?" If your thought is: *Oh, that was really stupid of me*, you can immediately ask yourself: *Is that true? Was that stupid of me? Am I stupid?* Of course that's not true. By asking those questions, you have interrupted the thought pattern, and now you can interject something that feels more loving to yourself.

The third method is to develop a true curiosity of discovering unconditional love. Really watch for it out in the world and catch people doing love right. Watch people being appreciative, saying kind things to one another, and also catch yourself doing things right. When you do something really good, such as giving your time to a friend in pain, you may think that that's just the way you are, and that's just what you do. But that's not what everybody does. It is a beautiful thing about you, and so you might catch yourself and say: *That was a really nice thing for me to do. I do make the people I love my priorities, and I love myself for that.* Be curious about what love looks like in the world. If you learn something from a way that someone else expresses unconditional love, try to duplicate that in your life.

Loving yourself is not about being self-absorbed, conceited, or egotistical. Recognize that loving yourself is actually the opposite. Love is all-encompassing. If you love yourself, you want to share more of yourself with others. Love enhances relationships in many ways. It enhances your relationship with yourself, makes you feel lighter, happier, more supported, and more stable.

It also enhances other relationships because if you come to another relationship from a place of love, you are able to give more in that relationship. When you experience love for yourself, you now have a reference point so you can identify what love feels like and what it looks like when other people are trying to give it to you. You already have the practice of receiving it because you are receiving it from yourself. You've developed the tools to express it to yourself, and therefore, to others. You have learned how to feel compassion for and be kind to yourself. You have learned how to listen to your inner voice. You have learned all those skills that make you feel loved. Now that you have those skills and tools, you can use them in relationships with other people to help make them feel loved. You can listen to their needs. You can hear what they are saying. You can see the way that they express love. You can have more compassion for them and more sympathy or empathy or whatever it is that they are needing. Loving becomes a natural, organic process.

Now that you are able to express love, you can receive it. I am not just talking about romantic relationships. I am talking about relationships with your children, with your parents, with your friends, with your colleagues, with your siblings, with your pets, with everyone and everything. This shows up in every single part of your life because relationships are such a big part of who you are. If you love yourself, you are not afraid to be yourself. You come into a relationship saying, "I am okay with me, and I would very much love that you are okay with me also. But if we are not a match, that's fine." There's no convincing people to love you. There's no convincing yourself to love somebody else. There is simply an exchange of love and energy. That doesn't mean that if you have conflict with somebody, you can't love them. Conflict is a natural part of all authentic relationships. It simply means that I accept you, respect you, love you, trust you, and whatever happens here, we can do that for one another.

Your angry outbursts are going to look different now. Your interactions are going to look different. Your conflict resolution is going to look different. Your way of communicating is going to *be* different, and so is your way of expressing appreciation and love. When you come to a relationship with that sort of authenticity, you are going to just express yourself very, very differently. You are also going to feel differently about the way people express themselves to you. Your reactions to them are going to be more grounded and less reactive. You are going to feel more stable, and you won't take disagreements as personally. You will do what's right for you regardless of what anyone else thinks.

After I got out of college, I started thinking about settling down. I knew my parents wanted me to marry someone of Indian descent, and that seemed to makes sense. But then I started going out with the people who should have been good matches for me, and I made up my mind about one thing. Marrying an Indian man was not even an option. I had grown up under the oppressive power of stereotypes, and I saw most Indian men as controlling. I would not be held down, and certainly not by a life partner.

In those days I wasn't sure about a lot, but if I was certain of one thing, it was this. More than anything, I wanted to be free to be my own person. Free of other people's opinions of me. Free of others' expectations. Free of being controlled. Free to be the me that I wanted to be.

The Indian men I dated were looking for traditional housewives. I wanted it all, a life of adventure and travel. Our goals and ideas were completely at odds.

However, when I met David—a super kind, open-minded, eager, white professional—I didn't even consider him a prospect. Sure, he treated me with the utmost respect. Sure, he wasn't the least bit controlling. Sure, he always acted as if I were an equal. And sure, he wasn't Indian. But there just wasn't that spark, that special something.

We went out a few times, but I knew that he wasn't the one. Still, he waited. He never pushed. But he waited.

He waited for six long months. He never made me uncomfortable, he didn't ask me out incessantly, and he was always respectful. I knew he wanted to be with me more than anything else.

Then one day, my phone rang.

"Hey! I didn't get my invitation."

Somehow David had heard about the birthday party I was throwing myself. I hadn't even considered inviting him.

"Oh, no!" I was so embarrassed. "It must have gotten lost in the mail," I lied.

So David came to my Murder Mystery Birthday Party. He played full out. He was charming. He was full of life, full of laughter. He made me feel so special. All of a sudden, I realized that he was sexy.

David had to leave the party early, and as he said his goodbyes and moved toward the door, I heard myself thinking, *Wait a minute! You can't leave.*

I was hooked and soon realized David was my soulmate. We were married a year and a half later. I'll share in greater detail shortly about why we were unable to have children. Yet I needed a little one to love, and for me, that was a dog. David didn't share that desire because traveling was one of our big bliss points, and we didn't have room for a dog in our lives.

About five years into our marriage, I started to say, "Sweetie, I really want a dog. I really want a puppy." He would remind me, "We don't have the time for a puppy." Then a special occasion would come up, like Valentine's Day or our wedding anniversary, and I would, say "So Sweetie, what am I getting for our anniversary?"

In those days, David was not all that great at remembering special occasions, so this was my playful way of reminding him that this was important to me. It became kind of a running joke that he knew I would ask this question, and he would say, "You are getting a puppy."

I would then say, "Really?" and he would reply, "No, not really." The conversation was my way of asking him not to forget, and his way of saying, "I'm on it."

On our weekly date night about three weeks before one of our anniversaries, I said, "So, Baby, what am I getting for my anniversary?"

"A puppy," he replied.

"Really?" I said.

"Yes!" he exclaimed. "You actually are getting a puppy."

I have always loved Pomeranians, so my husband had started to do some research on Pomeranian rescues because I am also committed to rescuing. Our new dog had been through a lot of pain. Once a service animal, his owner died, and the poor little guy was abandoned twice. He needed some love, and this little dog was like a sponge for love. He and I attached immediately. He did have separation anxiety and his own emotional trauma, but he did not shut out my love because of his past. Every moment that I am with Pom Frite (pronounced *Pom Freet*) is a moment of love.

I had heard people say that you don't have any idea about what unconditional love is unless you've had a dog. At the time I hadn't believed them. But now I do. In Pom Frite's eyes I am perfect. He loves me just the way I am, without judgment. When I screw up, he always forgives me. I can count on him to love me no matter what. It's a crazy wonderful feeling that I had never experienced in such a pure form ever before. It now gives me a reference point for what it feels like, and what I can strive toward.

I have been very fortunate to have experienced a lot of love in my life. Even through the rough relationships, I always had some shining light of love in my life. But whether you have experienced love in your life to the degree you want or not does not determine how much love you can experience from now on. It starts from within. You can begin to love, whether it is a flower, a butterfly, or your dog. Love creates love, and it all starts with you loving you.

One of the things I've learned about in life is that you can't love unconditionally if you can't forgive. That could also mean holding a grudge or being resentful or angry. And the most important person to forgive is yourself. Because without that, you can't truly love yourself.

We'll talk more about this in another chapter, but everybody has things in their past that they would do differently, and the inability to change the past is why some people really wrestle with forgiveness. It's not about asking another person to forgive you. It's about asking yourself for forgiveness first. You might come up with examples of romantic relationships where you treated someone badly. Maybe you did something unethical in business, perhaps stole something from another person. You felt a scarcity mindset that drove you to do something that you would never dream of doing today.

One of the things a mentor of mine often says to me is: "If you are on a diet, and you ate pizza yesterday, can you change that you ate pizza yesterday? You can't. All you can change is what you are going to eat today and what you are going to eat tomorrow, but you can't change what you ate yesterday. So there is no sense in crying over that and beating yourself up. It happened. It is gone."

If you don't forgive yourself, you will continue to carry around the emotions that weigh you down, which prevent you from expressing love in the present and in the future. The emotions you are still expressing are shame and guilt, not love. The only way to fix things that you have done wrong in the past is to express love to the best of your capacity today.

"Bliss isn't circumstantial. It's a way of being."

~ **Moneeka Sawyer**

Chapter Six
Forgiveness

"It's one of the greatest gifts you can give yourself, to forgive.
Forgive everybody."

~ Maya Angelou

Bliss is our birthright. When we are born we are just a big bundle of unconditional love. But through life, we have experiences and we learn from society, our culture, and the people around us how to be. Part of what we learn is how to hold grudges, how to hate, how to withhold forgiveness. Because of that, we have to relearn how to forgive. The true art of forgiveness is to realize that no forgiveness is really necessary, that everything happens as it is supposed to.

What is forgiveness? Does it mean admitting that you are wrong? Is it a sign of weakness? If you forgive, do you lose the upper hand? How many times do we decide not to forgive somebody? Maybe we feel they don't deserve it. What's the point? These are all important questions to answer because I believe forgiveness is the ultimate spiritual detox.

Forgiveness: A Spiritual Detox

What is a detox? A detox is a process in which one rids the body of toxic or unhealthy substances. When we talk about a spiritual detox we are talking about the process of clearing toxins out of the spiritual, emotional, and energy bodies.

The process of forgiveness is to stop feeling anger toward someone who has done something wrong to you, to stop blaming, and to give up your resentment toward them. I believe forgiveness is also key to gaining control of our lives from past hurts that we have experienced. When we carry resentment or anger, we are carrying those heavy emotions inside of us. When we forgive we are getting rid of those toxic thoughts and emotions. We are not condoning someone's actions. We don't need to continue a relationship with that person or even say anything to that person. When you forgive, you are releasing your feelings about those actions that have hurt you and releasing the emotions that are weighing you down. Negative emotions such as anger, resentment, rage, and spite all eat you up from the inside. They are slow killers and will eventually destroy you. However, if you release them, you create room for more positive emotions that feed, nourish, and nurture you. They give you more of what you want in life. That's why I think of forgiveness as a spiritual detox.

What if we don't feel like forgiving?

A lot of us don't want to forgive because we believe that there were very real harms or wrongs done against us. It is really hard to look at some situations and even think about forgiving. For instance, if someone has been through a huge trauma such as sexual molestation or physical violence, it is really hard to think about forgiveness, especially if the person who committed those wrongs has not been punished. In those cases, not wanting to forgive is very real. Those wrongs are very real.

On a completely different level, there are wrongs that are done to us by our parents, by our siblings, by our best friends, and by our lovers that would never end up in a court of law. Wrongs happen every single day and sometimes we feel like we don't want to forgive those things. We feel we have a right to be angry about them. I don't want to trivialize the fact that bad things happen and that they are very real, very painful.

Whether something goes punished or unpunished, whether some wrong was real or not real, whether you perceive a wrong or were actually physically wronged, whatever has happened is circumstance. However, *you* get to choose how to react to those circumstances. You get to choose how much power to give to the circumstances and to the people involved in those circumstances. If you don't want to forgive you can make that choice. It is yours to make. You just need to keep in mind that when you are holding a grudge against someone it hurts you more than it hurts them. You need to understand that each of us has to live with ourselves and look at ourselves in the mirror every day. Whoever has wronged you has to live with their own way of being and their own choices, but you don't have to continue to live with them inside of you for your entire life. You get to live with you, and you can eject them.

Thus, it is important for you, personally, for your "self," to let go. Letting go is not about forgetting. It is about releasing the chains others have around you. As long as you don't forgive them, they can tug those chains and drag you around with them even if they are not in your life anymore. Just the memory of them, just that grudge, anger, spite, and that need for revenge binds you to them. When you forgive, you are breaking those chains around you. You are releasing their power over you and taking your power back where it belongs. Notice forgiveness is not really about the other person. It doesn't have anything to do with the other person. It is really all about you and gaining back your own freedom from all these horrible emotions.

Here's an example. Let's say you have met a really, really great guy. And you are in love with him, and everything is going amazingly. One day he says to you, "Baby, I really want to move in together."

You, inexplicably, get completely triggered by this, and lash back with, "I don't ever want to live with someone until I am married. I can't believe you just asked me that. Don't you respect me?" In short, you go off on a rampage. From his perspective he is just saying, "I am willing to make the next level of commitment to you, and I want to move in." Let's just say in your past history you moved in with somebody and he started taking you for granted. He wanted to be able to live with you and you felt that you were being used for sex and to take care of him. Maybe he even cheated on you and the relationship ended terribly. You tried to kick him out of your house but he wouldn't go. So you had to move out. All this trauma took place because you two lived together. Now this new guy has no idea about that trauma, but he is in love with you and is thinking about marrying you. For him, part of the movement toward marriage is to live together for a little while. He is coming to you with an expression of love, but you have all this upset and trauma around the idea of living with someone. You haven't forgiven your ex for all that happened during your last relationship. Now, you bring all of that trauma into this new relationship. It doesn't belong there, but you have brought it there because you haven't taken the time to forgive your ex, let go, learn your lessons, and move forward so that you can be fully available to this new person in a more appropriate, open way.

All of this spite, anger, and holding grudges can misdirect your life and cause you to have certain behaviors that are inappropriate for your current circumstances. This does not help you achieve your goals. In this particular case, let's say you want a loving relationship. You want to get married. You want this person to stay with you forever. Yet, your actions push him away. Those actions are completely based on bitterness and anger. They are not based on current situations and the reality of the circumstances. Your inability to forgive blinds you from being able to see the truth.

When you are able to forgive you will be able to remove those blinders so that you can see everything around you for what it really is.

The misunderstandings of forgiveness

I mentioned before that forgiveness has nothing to do with condoning. It also is not about reconciliation. Because you forgive, that does not mean that you have to start up a relationship with that person again. You don't have to go and tell them that you have forgiven them. If that person is out of your life, it may be better that they stay out of your life. It doesn't have anything to do with that person. The forgiveness is really all about you and what's going on inside of you.

A common cliché is "forgive and forget." Because of that too many people think forgiving is about forgetting. On the contrary, sometimes it's really important to not forget. It's important to learn the lessons from the experiences you had. If you were to just forget, then you wouldn't keep the lessons. You would lose the wisdom that you can extract from the incident. Forgiving is not about forgetting. Forgiving is about releasing. You should take the lesson from the experience and the wisdom that it offers you so that you can move forward in your life on your path. Why hold a grudge when you got what you needed from that lesson?

Sometimes people believe that forgiveness means that we won't pursue action against a perpetrator. So if you forgive them, then that means that you don't have to seek legal punishment of a rapist, for instance. Or if a company has wronged you and there is a class action suit, forgiving them means that you don't get involved in the class action suit. I don't believe this is true either. Actions often need to be and should be taken against people who have wronged you. The question you must ask yourself is: What is the difference between vengeance and justice? Are you trying to get back at somebody or are you trying to seek the rightful path of justice? For example. If you forgive a murderer, you are not saying that murder is okay. You are just letting go of the burning fury inside of you so it doesn't eat you up. The court case to seek justice of the accused will still continue. That person took an action and there will be consequences, but you do not need to bind your own emotions to that process. You can be emotionally free of that person right away.

The Principles of Forgiveness

The first principle of forgiveness is to accept yourself and all your humanness. Before you can forgive anyone else, you need to be able to forgive yourself, and the very first step to that is to accept that we are all human. We have our failings and our flaws and we have lessons that we need to learn. Accepting this about ourselves helps us to be kinder and more compassionate to ourselves when we screw up. And we all screw up.

We all carry guilt, fear, sadness, and regret. We all carry those things because we, too, feel as if we have wronged and hurt other people. That's why you must recognize that we are human. In every given situation you did the very best that you could, given the information you had. That instance, circumstance, and those times are gone, and now your responsibility is to move forward with more kindness and more compassion toward yourself and toward others. You can't actually offer these things fully to others unless you can offer them to yourself.

The second principle is to learn to accept all others in their humanness. Once you can accept your own humanness, you can more easily accept the humanness of others. You can start to understand that we are all just doing the very best that we can in this life. We all screw up whether we mean to or not and it is not necessary to carry a grudge around about other people's screw ups. They have their own lessons to learn, but we don't need to carry their mistakes around with us.

The more responsible you are, the harder you can be on yourself and others, and the harder it may be for you to forgive yourself and others. This all really comes back to you. You might notice a theme here. Being a responsible person is great, but anything taken to an extreme is detrimental. Your attitude is picked up by others. How can you expect them to be kind and forgiving to you, when you can't even be kind and forgiving to yourself?

If your standards are so high you are constantly beating yourself up for not meeting them, are those standards serving you? Perhaps those standards are showing you what you and others are doing wrong, while missing out on what they are doing right. Acknowledge that being responsible is a beautiful characteristic. Don't let it distract you from the beauty in yourself and others.

The third principle is to realize that what someone else has done to us has more to do with them and less to do with us. When someone does something terrible to you, sometimes they don't even know what they are doing is terrible. They may be unconscious and unaware and they themselves are just floundering through their lives. When they screw up it may not have anything to do with you. You may perceive that you were wronged and carry that action that they did unconsciously around with you for the rest of your life. And for what purpose? It never had anything to do with you in the first place. It was all about them and their circumstances. They were on a different path and not as aware as you are. Maybe someone stole something from you. Maybe someone betrayed you at work in order to get a promotion. Maybe they needed that promotion because they wanted to be able to send a child to preschool. Maybe they were taught at home to succeed at any cost. Maybe they were so caught up in their own needs and fears that they were not looking at what is happening around them. All of that had nothing to do with you.

The fourth principle is to accept that you are here for a particular purpose and your purpose will be supported by a series of lessons. The gems you can take away from the ugly things that have happened in your life are knowledge, learning, and wisdom. Once you have those, you can let go of all the rest—the anger, hate, resentment, and spite.

The fifth principle is to not use grudges as excuses. When we hold onto a grudge or we are not willing to forgive, we hold on to negative emotions of anger, hate and resentment. We often are using these things as an excuse to not learn our lessons. It can be easier to carry a grudge around and be a victim than to take responsibility for what you need to learn from an incident. Anger, resentment, spite, and hate are all distractors from self-examination. It is important that you learn to not distract yourself because those distractions don't serve you. They continue to perpetuate these emotions that hold you down and hold you back.

The sixth principle is knowing it is never too late to forgive. If you are in your mid-forties and you have a whole lifetime of bitterness, anger, and unhappiness, maybe it is showing up in your body and you are sick and tired. You've grown accustomed to it and figure it's too late to change. It is never too late. We can always start. Forgiveness can happen at any time and at any point in your life whether you are five or 105. It doesn't matter where you are in your life or what you have experienced. It is not too late. If you will do the work and give the forgiveness, you can still reap the benefits. They are all available to you.

So get started on it. That is the very first step you must take. Nothing can happen in life unless you take that first step. No matter how huge the pain seems. No matter how old it is or how deeply rooted it is in your being, there is no way to get through it and get the benefits of forgiveness unless you take the first step. That is your path to feeling lighter, more joyful, and to living bliss.

The second step is give yourself room to breathe and be human. It is okay to lose your temper, to get angry, to not want to forgive. It is okay to do all of those things, but just forgive yourself because forgiveness will be hard. Understand that this is all part of the process, that regressions happen, and that they are part of what you need to experience in order to get to the end. None of this work is linear. Nothing that I have talked about in this book is linear. Everything has its fits and starts. Everything has its moments where you feel like saying, "Wow. I really got that!" And then there are regressions where you have to reexamine. You are re-tested. You are re-learning. It is all part of the process.

Instead of beating yourself up for a regression, instead of beating yourself up for feeling anger that you thought that you already worked through, take a deep breath, accept that you are human and that this is part of the process. Let it go, and take the next step.

I have been blessed with amazing, amazing parents, but like every other parent, they screwed up many times. Many of those screw ups affected me deeply and I went through a forgiveness process until I thought I was past each issue. But oh no! Sometime later, I would have a conversation with Mom or Dad and I would be triggered again. That thing would come up, and I would blow up over it again. Later, I would go back and rework through that issue until I stopped being triggered.

I believe that each person who is or becomes important in our lives is here to teach us lessons that help us along our spiritual path. Sometimes there are layers and layers that we need to work through with regard to forgiveness because the people that we need to forgive had many lessons to teach us. The lessons that they were there to teach us were so deep that as we peel away each layer, we see a little bit more that is needed underneath it. All of these are opportunities for learning, and the deeper we go, the more we understand.

When working with clients, I am frequently reminded that forgiveness is one of those things that people don't want to do. Oh sure, it's nice to talk about, and it's talked about a lot. But it is actually a really difficult thing to do until you have done it a few times and realize how much your life improves when you do.

I might take a client through a forgiveness exercise and at the end of the session they feel as if they have gone really deep. They feel a release and they are so much more at peace.

Maybe they worked through an issue with their husband or

wife. Then, they will tell me that they went home and their husband or wife did the same thing again, and they got triggered and lost their temper. Does this mean the client failed? Not at all. It means only that they have gone through one layer but there is still that trigger. That trigger is still there for a reason. Let's do it again. Let's get to the next place, the next thing that that trigger is setting off. Maybe the first trigger is: *You are not listening to me.* Maybe the second trigger is: *You never help me.* Maybe the next trigger is: *You are always talking over me.* But as you keeping going deeper and you notice that he keeps triggering you, maybe at the very end of it all the trigger is: *I don't believe you love me.* Now, let's go even a little bit deeper. *Do I even love myself? Am I worthy?* It's unlikely you'll go deep down to that very core belief that's holding you down at the very beginning. It is too deep and covered in so many layers. Sometimes you just need to take those layers a little bit at a time. Whatever you can psychologically and emotionally handle is what you work though and you need to just keep working until you get to the root of it. Because, when you get to the root of it is when true transformation happens.

This is a process. Hopefully, after reading this chapter you are going to start working on your forgiveness practice tomorrow… and the next day, and next week, and next month, and next year. As I said, this is the ultimate detox. In order to go really deep and get big results, you need to keep at it.

Some days you are going to be able to focus on it and go through the process. Other days, you may not have the time or the energy, and you need a break. That's perfectly okay. Through all of this, be kind to yourself and recognize that your goal is forgiveness and unconditional love. Wherever you are at any given moment, whether you are taking a break and can't think about this anymore, or you are heavily in it and you are doing deep forgiveness work on a particular person in your life, understand what the goal is. The goal is to achieve your own personal freedom so that you can experience bliss and be able to express unconditional love out into the world.

The seventh principle is admitting that things are what they are. We can't ignore events in reality. If you turn your back on them, if you try not to look at them, if you try to hide them from your conscious or your subconscious, they will continue to haunt you. It is really important to admit that, excuse the language here, shit happens. And it did happen. Whatever it was, whatever you are feeling upset about, it did happen. You have to admit and acknowledge that. You cannot pretend it didn't happen. The next step is to accept that it happened, that it was there, and that it happened for a reason. Take your lesson from that. When you admit it, you look at it. When you accept it, you can integrate it. I am not saying that I want you to integrate the horrible feelings that came with that, but I want you to integrate the lessons and the wisdom that you learned from the incident. When you do, you can move on and evolve as a more enlightened, fulfilled, joyful person. You'll be more capable of making good decisions and good choices. You'll be more capable of helping others. You'll be more capable of giving and receiving love.

Forgiving Yourself

Sometimes the person you need to forgive the most is yourself. Suppose the voice in your head says, "I am not good enough." This is a thought that can be very persistent for many of us. Remember, Forgiveness is about being aware. That voice in your head that's saying that you are not good enough may never go away. It is important that you don't maintain a grudge against yourself for that. In other words, don't beat yourself up for this thought that keeps going on in your head with that same old message. Maybe you feel angry because it has controlled you. Maybe it has held you down. Maybe it has made it so that you can't do the things that you want to do. Maybe it has held you back from your vision and you feel really angry and frustrated with yourself for that.

Instead of beating yourself up over your own critical thoughts, learn to just accept this piece of yourself. Understand that it is going to be with you. Just notice it. Don't try to punish yourself for it. Don't try to punish it. Just buckle it in safely on the bus of your life and take it with you. Accept it as a part of who you are and make peace with it. The more that we struggle against ourselves, the worse things get. As we accept ourselves and love ourselves, everything becomes easier in general.

Let me confess that I have been extremely hard on myself my entire life. I am definitely a perfectionist, so I have found that instead of looking at the things that I did right, I consistently look at the things I have done wrong. When I was seventeen and applying to universities, I got waitlisted at a couple of the universities that I really, really wanted to get into. I was so upset about it that I thought that I wasn't good enough as a person. I thought I was a failure.

Harvard. Stanford. UCLA. Wharton. Berkeley.

This was my college wish list. In spite of my heartbreaking school experiences, I was good in school, and knowing I could attend a top university made me feel better about myself. I had applied to all five, but only two had sent me acceptance letters.

This was unacceptable. I felt betrayed by the one thing I thought I had on my side, my academic success.

I expected to be accepted at all five universities. I wanted to make my own choice. It had never occurred to me that any of these schools would tell me I wasn't good enough.

Although Stanford didn't have an undergraduate program in business, it was the one school I cared about the most. It was close to home and had the lowest acceptance rate of any of the colleges I had applied to. To be accepted there would have been my biggest achievement.

One day, I got home from dance and saw the letter from Stanford sitting on the kitchen table. I ripped it open and read these fateful words: *Thank you for applying. You are on the wait list.*

This didn't make any sense to me. Wait list? Why wait list? I don't understand.

So I called them.

In fact, I called them every single day.

That poor receptionist in the Admissions Office must have dreaded answering the phone every time it rang. Every day I called, and every day she told me, "I'm sorry, but I can't tell you why you were put on the wait list."

Every day I'd insist she give me an answer, and every day she put me through to one of the admission counselor's voice mails. Day after day after day.

Soon, another letter arrived from Stanford. Apparently, the counselors were getting tired of hearing my voice:

Dear Moneeka, I am writing to let you know that you were put on the wait list because your letters of recommendation were not as strong as we would have liked. But please don't worry. A certain percentage of students who are accepted don't come to Stanford, so you may still get in. And even if you don't get in this year, don't lose hope. You can still apply again next year.

The letter fell from my hand. That first sentence still rang in my ears: How could my letters of recommendation not be strong enough? This made absolutely no sense to me.

I needed answers.

So I picked up the phone and called the Stanford Admissions Office yet again.

"Yes. Yes, I did get the letter.

"Yes. Yes, I did read it…. But I don't understand. Can you send me a copy of my recommendation letters?

"I understand that this isn't usually done, but... Yes. Yes. I understand that it's highly unusual.

"Well, were all my letters a problem? I see.

"Well, can you send me the one letter that was a problem? Oh, that's against university policy?"

In the end, the receptionist held firm. There was no way that I was going to see that letter that was preventing me from getting into Stanford

So I did the only sensible thing a high-achieving senior who needed answers could do. I drove to Stanford University.

If I was a force to be reckoned with on the phone, I was a hurricane in person. I don't know if it was my persistence or my panic that won the day, but that receptionist had pity on me. She went to the filing cabinet, pulled out that manila folder with my name on it, and showed me the "recommendation" that stood between me and getting into Stanford.

I couldn't believe it.

"Moneeka is a very, very good student," the letter read. "However, she's very much lacking in leadership and social skills. She has very few friends and has no involvement in anything other than academics."

My eyes welled up. "But, but, this is a blatant lie," I said to no one in particular. "How could she write this about me?"

The letter was from my favorite teacher, Mrs. Baldridge who taught Honors History. She was the reason I had been called "teacher's pet" for so long. Not only was she my favorite teacher, I considered her my friend.

I was in complete shock. Even more, I was crushed.

My mind immediately went back to the beginning of my junior year, right after I had returned from my school year in India. I set up a meeting with my guidance counselor to talk about my future plans for college. I was highly optimistic. After all, I was a straight-A student and destined to be class valedictorian.

"It's not enough," Mrs. Thornton said.

She explained to me that to get in the very best schools, I needed to have more than academics. I needed to have extracurricular activities that show involvement and leadership with my peers.

"I understand," I said. "But I dance. I dance at the studio four hours after school every day."

"It's not enough," she said.

She convinced me. So we sat together and made a plan.

German Club. Mathematics Club. Creative Writing Club. Choir.

I actually started new clubs, and I was a leader in the rest. I ran for Junior Class Vice President and won. The next year, I was Senior Class President. All on top of going to my honors classes at 7 a.m. each day and dancing for four-plus hours a night after school.

So when I read those words about my not having any extracurricular activities, it made absolutely no sense to me. It wasn't true!

Reading that I had no social life and had no friends—the very issues that marked my young life throughout my entire school experience—hurt me. But had been changed with positive thinking and smiles after my return from India. I was completely flabbergasted. Confused. Hurt. Angry.

Perhaps I should have gone back to Mrs. Baldridge and confronted her. To ask her to explain herself and account for her lies about me. To ask her to rewrite her letter—or call Stanford and admit her wrongdoing.

But I didn't do any of those things.

I had spent most of my high school years trying to fit in, trying to be liked. Now, here I was, with my favorite teacher, someone I *knew* accepted me and liked me, and she had totally undermined my chances to reach my goal.

Just like that, I learned no matter how much someone likes you, he or she can still stab you in the back.

However, this experience was a gift, a revelation. People are not always trustworthy, sure, but more important, I didn't have to be victimized. I was in control over my own life. I didn't have to be liked to be successful. I could choose to act. And I could write my own future.

So I went to my Honors Algebra teacher and asked him to write me a new letter of recommendation to Stanford.

When the letter from Stanford finally came in the spring of my senior year, I wrote back.

"Thank you for reconsidering me…

"But no thanks. I'm going to Berkeley."

Years later, I was thinking back to those days and how I beat myself up. I realized that Berkeley was exactly the place that I was supposed to go. It was a perfect fit for me. The universe had it under control. It got me into the place where I needed to go to learn the things that I needed to learn for the life path that I wanted to follow. So, instead of beating myself up and being in judgement about how incompetent I was or what a failure I was, what if I had looked at it differently?

Even though I got wait-listed at Stanford and Harvard, those schools didn't have an undergraduate business program, which is what I wanted to do. What if I had been kind to myself instead of beating myself up so much that I didn't enjoy my last year of high school. What if I had said, "I am smart enough and I am going to do whatever I can to get into the schools of my choice. And then, whatever school I go to, I am going to make it the best experience

I possibly can." How would that have changed me? How much more self-confidence would I have had going into business school if I felt good about myself rather than beating myself up?

I want to tell you the story about my mom. This was the ultimate lesson in forgiveness to me. My birthday is in the first week of May and often falls on Mother's Day. When that happens my mom and I always celebrate my birthday and Mother's Day together. We will usually go out one day together, just the girls, and she and I get to really connect. It is such a special time for me that I look forward to it all year.

About five or six years ago, Mom and I went out to get our nails done, and as we were sitting there getting our pedicures, we were very quiet for a few minutes. Then Mom turned to me and said, "Moneeka, I am so very sorry for all the times I let you down and all the times I hurt you." Her eyes were full of tears and there was so much pain in them. All I could think of was: What are you talking about?

She had been carrying around this pain and beating herself up for years about what she had done wrong to me. This broke my heart because I understand that my mom loves me more than any other human being on the planet. She has always done the very best that she possibly could, and despite whatever anger and upset we have had with each other, it was never her intention to hurt me, ever. I have been through my own journey of forgiveness with regard to her, and I have been through my own journey of forgiveness with regard to myself and what I may have done to her. But here she was at the age of seventy-six, crying because she wasn't able to forgive herself. Literally, I sat there holding her hand as she sobbed about what a horrible mother she had been. All I could say was, "Mom, we love each other. There is nothing you should feel sorry about." There has never truly been any forgiveness required, because I know that she has always done the very best that she could and that she loves me deeply.

Many times we'll never get to hear an "I am sorry." We may also never get to say "I am sorry." In both of these cases, we need to learn to forgive. Because if we don't have the power of forgiveness, we'll never get closure. I think in this particular case Mom and I together got closure for each other with each other. But many of us never get that opportunity. For instance, if a loved one passes away, we are often left with so many things that we didn't get to say. As I mentioned above, maybe we didn't get to say "I'm sorry." Maybe we didn't get to clear the air about things that have hurt us in the past. Maybe we never got to ask why they did certain things. In this case we will never get to experience closure with them. The only closure we can ever get is to learn to forgive for ourselves. That is the only way we can move on.

What I learned from that experience is that all of us are limited by our own perceptions. For instance, my mom thought she knew the whole situation. She thought she knew how I was feeling and what I was thinking. But she has got her own pain. And this pain was influencing her perceptions and keeping her in pain. I also really got that she has always done the very best that she could. None of the things that she has done that I may have perceived as mean were meant to be mean. What I wanted to say to my mom, and I have said it since then, is that the world can be a really hard place. It can also be a really joyful place and life can be a huge adventure. But there really is a lot about the world that is difficult. So be kind to yourself. Here on this planet the only person we really have to be on our side one hundred percent of the time is ourselves. When the world is hard on you, it is really important to be easy on yourself. You need to forgive yourself for your failings and love and accept yourself unconditionally. Only then can you truly learn to forgive others and reap the benefits that forgiveness brings.

Forgiveness is acceptance of what happened, understanding that it was supposed to happen, getting to a place where you believe you are a better person because it happened, and finally to make peace with what happened and know that everything is okay.

Before we finish this chapter, I'd like to give you some exercises that you can do on your own to get you started on this path of forgiveness. Forgiveness is a huge topic and there are lots of beautiful ways to explore it and to expand your capacity to forgive. Here are two to get you started.

Exercise #1: Conversation

Close your eyes and picture somebody you are currently holding a grudge against or have had some sort of unresolved conflict with.

Do you have that person in mind?

Next write out who this person is, what the event was that caused this tension between you, and how you feel about it.

Finally, and most important, in your own words and in your own way, try to forgive that person. Write all this down.

Now, since you have this written out, do you think you would be willing to talk about it? I suggest you talk about it into a mirror. Start by reading what you wrote and go with whatever comes up for you. Keep talking into the mirror until you have absolutely nothing left to say.

Then, if you feel up to it, talk about what you would like from this person. What is it that you need?

You may never get that thing you need, but acknowledging it shows you what you've been waiting for. What you've been holding out for. Once you know that, you can release that expectation and release your attachment to that person completely.

Remember, forgiveness comes from within. Learn to forgive and to move on.

Exercise #2: Affirmations

This exercise is to help you forgive yourself. On a sticky note, write the following affirmations:

(Your name), I forgive you for _____.

(Your name), I love that you _____.

(Your name), I appreciate that you have _____.

Once you have written these things out, put the post-it note on your mirror and look at it every time you look in the mirror. Repeat the affirmations to yourself and give yourself the time to feel the impact of the words. Do this until you feel like the sentiments have become a part of your being. If you like, you can then start a new set of affirmations. Remember, loving and forgiving yourself is the single most important thing you need to do to feel true bliss. Keep this as a tool you can use frequently to increase the bliss in your life.

Chapter Seven
Self-Responsibility and Choices

"Be miserable. Or motivate yourself.
Whatever has to be done, it's always your choice."

~ **Wayne Dyer**

We have the power to make choices in our lives. We have the power to make our lives what we want them to be.

Every single thing that we do in life is a choice. Every single choice that we make has a consequence. It is really easy to blame someone else for the circumstances that made you make a choice. But the reality is people and circumstances are not something you can control. The only thing you have any power over is yourself, and it is only that power that allows you to live a joyful, blissful life. You can't influence the world to give you the things that are going to make you joyful. All we have is you. Life presents challenges to show who you are by the choices that you make. You develop your character. You develop your life. You develop your strengths and power through the choices that you make and by how you deal with the consequences that come from those choices.

One day I was having lunch with my closest, oldest friend Tania. Her mom is a brilliant doctor but a scattered personality. She is good with her patients, but she has little common sense.

Tania's younger brother is autistic. Between the two of them, they generate a lot of crises. Tania feels a huge sense of responsibility to take care of her family, each crisis, and all the everyday issues that come up. She is running around constantly helping her mom clean the house and get things organized. They are trying to put together a trust fund for her little brother because he can't take care of himself. She is rushing her little brother to his therapy sessions and her mom to the hospital, and doing all of these things that "a good Indian daughter" would do. I can completely relate to her. I have to say I actually agree with her choices, but the thing is that they are *her* choices. When I tell her this, she says "Okay. Moneeka, if I don't do it, who is going to do it?" Good question. Who *is* going to do it? *They* are going to do it. They have been doing it. Her mom didn't get to be seventy-six years old not being able to take care of herself and her son. Most of the setting up of care for her son is already done. Of course, the fact that her daughter is helping her is a huge boon for her. It is also good for my friend's spirit to be helping her family. This is one of her core cultural values. But when it becomes an obligation and something that makes her crazy and exhausted and hating her life, it is not serving her. The reality is that *she* is making those choices.

She is not dealing with the circumstances. She is making a choice and then resenting that she made that choice. She could be saying, "I am making this choice because this is what my value system is. How can I make this fit into my life? How can I make myself okay with this?" Instead, she is saying, "I hate this. Why can't they take care of themselves? Why can't they figure it out? This is making me crazy. I am exhausted. I feel so sick."

That's what happens when you blame other people as opposed to taking responsibility for your choices. In her case, she could accept that instead of her family being a distraction from her life, her family *is* her life. Do you see the difference?

She would still be doing everything she is currently doing, but her attitude would be very different. Then, every time she got frustrated, she would tell herself, "I am here because I want to be, I am here because I want to be. This is really frustrating, but I am here because I want to be." That's the reality of life. There are a lot of things that we do that we don't love doing and they can be frustrating. They can cause stress and upset. Everything in life is not going to be fun, and every choice that you make is not going to be fun for you. But it is your choice, and acknowledging that will empower you. I told my friend every single time she gets into that place of "Why can't they take care of themselves?" to remind herself that they *can* take care of themselves, but she is there because she chooses to be, and her help is valuable to them. It will make life much easier for her.

We all make bad choices sometimes. Take responsibility for making that bad choice, take the lesson from it, and try to move forward with that lesson. Hopefully, you won't make that same bad choice the next time. If you do, learn from it, and *then* hopefully you won't make that choice again. The more you take responsibility and the more you look at your choices as opportunities to learn and grow, the sooner you will stop making the bad choices. One of the most important things to remember is when you make a bad choice, do not begrudge yourself that choice. Forgive yourself for making it. Accept that it was a choice that you made. It was the best choice that you could have made based on the knowledge that you had at that time. Now that you have more knowledge, you have the opportunity to make different choices. Keep going forward. And don't hold a grudge against yourself.

Do you want to have power over your choices in your life or do you want circumstances to dictate what your life is going to look like and how much joy you get to experience?

Recently our economy went really, really bad, and a lot of people lost their homes because they were over mortgaged. Many lost their jobs, and horrible things happened to people's lives. Let's say you were one of those people, and you started drinking because it was too difficult to deal with. It always starts off with one glass of wine at night just to relax and calm your nerves. Then you need two glasses. Things get worse, and you increase your drinking. Now you are black-out drunk every night, and you are miserable. Further, you are not able to succeed at finding a new job. Your relationships may not be working anymore. Life has turned into a nightmare, and it is all because the darn economy turned bad. Your mantra is: *I hate our president, and I hate the economy. I wish Social Security started paying earlier.* Those are toxic thoughts. What if instead, you took responsibility for your own choices and actions? What if you took a look at your industry? Do you want to stay there anymore? If not, maybe you want to get some new training because you were sick of your job anyway. Why don't you retrain during these couple of years? Hopefully, more jobs will open up in the new industry that you are looking at, and you can move forward. In this case, you are making choices to empower yourself and to grow, no matter what the circumstances are. As you empower yourself and you grow, new choices appear for you. You are able to see things differently because you are seeing things from the position of having control over this situation in your life. It would be better to have thoughts like "I am going to make good choices and I am going to make this work", as opposed to, "I hate the president. I hate our country. I hate that I am not getting Social Security." Those negative thoughts are not going to serve you. You have a choice on how you are going to react to the circumstances of a recession.

You have a choice about how you react to everything. Don't allow circumstances to dictate your choices. You can take control of your life, your joy, and your experiences. You have that power.

Chapter Eight
Tough Choices

"Decision is the spark that ignites action. Until a decision is made, nothing happens.... Decision is the courageous facing of issues, knowing that if they are not faced, problems will remain forever unanswered."

~ Wilfred A. Peterson

When David and I got married, we decided we were not going to have children. At that time, that choice really made sense for us. But as I got older, my maternal instincts kicked in, and I changed my mind. I needed to make a tough choice at that point. Should I bring it up and possibly lose my husband, or should I keep it inside and possibly regret it for the rest of my life. Sometimes we need to make really tough choices. I took a huge risk and decided to talk to David.

"But we agreed that we didn't want children," David said.

We were sitting on a bench in Paris waiting for the train to take us to Lyon.

"We also agreed that we would talk about it if I ever changed my mind," I replied.

We sat in silence for a while, not knowing how to move forward from there.

Thus began the first of many train station conversations about babies. At the time, we were living in Lyon, France, and David was always in a good mood when we were embarking on a new adventure. It seemed like the best time to engage him on the topic of starting a family.

So we had the conversation on train benches in Paris, Lyon, Carcassonne, Strasbourg, Nice, and many others. Eventually, David agreed. "All right," he said. "Let's try."

In Paris, we conceived.

I had no problem getting pregnant.

Just as I was completing my first trimester of my pregnancy in France, I miscarried.

Although I had a history of miscarriages, this was the first time David and I were intentional about starting a family. I was devastated. David, I suspect, was a little relieved.

When we got back to the States, I redoubled my efforts.

I tried everything to ensure that I would succeed: Traditional Western medicine. Fertility clinics. Hormone injections. Acupuncture. Energy work. Strict nutritional approaches.

It consumed our attention, our focus, our lives, and our resources. Fertility work is expensive.

"I don't think I can do this," David said one evening as we were having dinner at a restaurant.

I'm not sure if David just assumed that I would never carry a baby to full term, or if he didn't count on my commitment being so intense and so costly. In any event, he was done.

I looked at him with compassion and conviction. "You can't tell a woman she can't have children. You need to decide."

He did. And he left.

Our separation was short-lived. David returned after a couple of weeks.

"This is really stupid," he said. "I love you. I want to support you in this."

It was David's turn to choose his bliss, and he chose to connect his bliss to mine.

The doctor smeared the cold gel on my abdomen and moved the wand over and back, over and back.

I lay there, looking up at the white ceiling and the fluorescent lights. I had been on three months of complete bed rest, so I was all too familiar with lying down.

I was feeling really good about this pregnancy. Everything was aligned. Everything felt right. I had given myself until I turned forty-two to have a child. That birthday was just a few months away. This was it!

The doctor removed the wand and readjusted the position of the monitor. She put the wand back on my stomach and moved it around again.

She had a strained, tight look on her face.

"Doctor?"
She removed the wand and looked at me.

"I think we lost the heartbeat."

"What?"

"There is no heartbeat. I'm so very sorry."

It didn't register. This was my fourteenth pregnancy. Each one had ended in a miscarriage at the end of the first trimester.

"Oh, that must be so hard for you to tell people," was all I could say.

The doctor left the room. I just sat there. I sat there on the end of the examination table, shocked in a sterile white room with my dead baby on the screen. At least that's what it felt like.

I started to cry. Then, I couldn't cry at all.

I walked out of the medical center, got into my car, and then it came. I sat there in the parking lot and sobbed.

In my experience, after the miscarriage, the baby would be released the following week. It was always traumatic, but I knew what to expect.

A week passed, and then another. After three weeks, the doctor scheduled a DNC.

Weeks after the procedure, I was still in intense pain, both physical and emotional. I still felt my child inside of me, and the physical pain of their going in and yanking it out.

More time passed. I still couldn't sleep because I was in so much pain.

One night, I turned to David and said, "I just can't do this anymore. I have to find a way to be happy without a baby."

After my decision, the response from my family and friends was supportive but hard to take. I told my parents that we were going to stop trying, and they cried with me. They felt my sadness. They felt their own.

The conversations always turned to considering other options: Could you adopt? Could you get a surrogate?

I asked David, "If I really decided that I want to adopt, would you be all right with that?"

"Absolutely," he said.

Everyone knew how much I had tried to have a child. I was so maternal and invested.

But in the end, I decided that I was done.

"No," I would say. "No, no. I just lost fourteen children. I need to recover. I need to move on."

My well-meaning family and friends would say things like, "Are you sure?" and "Maybe you'll regret this."

In the end, although all these voices in my life were trying to support me, I had to stand up for myself and stop the conversation. It was time for some deep soul searching. It was time for some self-care.

The major turning point in my life came when, instead of relating to life as not being able to get what I thought I wanted, I decided to choose bliss.

Whether I ever had a child or not, I decided I would choose bliss.

This allowed me to reconcile what I thought I wanted with what I had—and with what I may never have.

Six months after that last miscarriage, my dear friend Paula called me and invited me to lunch.

"I had a dream about you last night," she said.

"Oh?"

"Yes. In my dream, we had a baby together," Paula said.

"What? What do you mean?"

Paula looked at me intently. "Moneeka, if you still want to have a baby, I would love to be your surrogate."

I started to cry. What an amazing gift from one of my closest friends.

I told her, "No," and we cried together.

It was in that moment, that I knew I had chosen bliss. As much as this loving offer to help could have brought a child into my life, I knew that I had made my decision. And my decision was not to have children.

When I knew that I had a viable option—a truly good option—to have my own biological child, and my heart still held to its resolve, I knew that I had made the right choice. It wasn't resignation. It was a positive stand, a decision to move forward for myself.

In that moment, I realized that we—you, I, everyone—get to make our choices and live with those choices. It is in the choosing where you will truly find your bliss.

Once I realized I was not going to be able to have a child, I became more involved with doing humanitarian work for Badarikashrama Vidyashala, a school in India for poor children.

I have been fundraising in the United States, have written a blog, and have done a lot of work for them, but I hadn't actually visited. I got the opportunity to go in 2015 and decided that while I was there I wanted to film a documentary about the school. During the filming I got to know the children and was able dig deep into their hopes and dreams.

Before I left for India, I had to prepare myself emotionally for the big questions. What if I fell in love with being around the children? What if my maternal instinct kicked in again? My husband and I had a lot of conversations about the following question again, "If I decide I want to adopt, is that going to be okay with you?" By the time I left for India his answer was, "Of course. If you decide you want to, we will adopt a child." I was as scared and excited as someone who suspects they may be pregnant.

I headed off to India and I loved the children. I loved their joy, loved their appreciation for the work we were doing. I loved how involved they were with their schooling and the way their parents were supporting them. It was such an amazingly beautiful experience for me. I was surprised to find that I never once felt like I wanted to adopt one of those children or that I needed to have a child. It was a validation that I had made the right choice for my spiritual path, and that I had moved on from the trauma that I had experienced with all my miscarriages. It felt clear that I had learned the lessons that I needed to learn.

There are still people who say to me, "Moneeka, are you sad you never had children?" or "Moneeka, you could still adopt." What I really want from the people who love me is an understanding that I went through my journey with regard to children. I have made a series of decisions. I want to live my life a certain way, and I want support for that life. I don't want to keep looking back. I don't want people feeling sorry for me because I never had children, because that's not my story. It's a part of my history, but it's not my life story. That's not my path. I could have adopted but chose not to. I have turned the page. It seems some people can't accept that. Others have an understanding of my choices and help me along my journey instead of trying to turn me back. This is the key. I made the choice to move on. I'm not angry with myself or anyone else for the decisions I've made. I've moved forward. I didn't allow circumstances or people to make me feel bad about my life. If you don't take responsibility you are allowing circumstances to make the choices for you.

Chapter Nine
Play and Creativity

"The ant is knowing and wise, but he doesn't know enough to take a vacation."

~ Clarence Day

This chapter took a couple of weeks to write because I was on vacation. That's right. I took a vacation while writing a book.

No, I wasn't putting off anything. It was time for a vacation and that's what I did. You might consider doing the same thing. People need this break. It has been proven many times that we function better after we allow ourselves some downtime. I'm certain that brain surgeons can't just operate on brains all day. They need to take breaks to rejuvenate their own brains before cutting into other people's. Whatever your career, you'll function better when you give yourself some downtime.

My husband, who is in computer programming, has been into computers since he was eight years old. It is his deepest passion and ceaseless fun to him. I have often said that his work is his mistress and I am his wife, because he loves his work so much. He can work all day and not be exhausted. It completely energizes him. Still, he does his work better if he takes vacations. That's just a fact. Because he works long days, he and I will often take a lunch and go out of the office. His boss told me that you can actually see visual proof of when he took a break for lunch and when he didn't. His work is better when he gives his brain a break. When you allow your brain to relax, it has more to offer you when you return to a task than when you strain at a problem all the time.

On our very first vacation together, my husband brought his work with him. Although his work makes him happy, I am a big advocate of no work while you are playing. So on our next vacation, he didn't bring work with him, and when he returned, his productivity practically doubled.

Why? Some of it was because he was happy to get back to it. Additionally, he had rested and allowed his mind to expand freely so that now when he looked at his programs, at the architecture, and at any problem, he was much more creative and more capable. He produced more in the first week after our vacation than he would normally have produced in a month.

He was the highest producer in the company while taking five weeks of vacation a year. He ended up being the highest paid person in the company because of his productivity. I could try to argue about the benefits of vacation or I could simply point to my husband. Case closed. Good managers understand the importance of vacations. If you haven't been taking vacations, you're not doing yourself or your business any favors.

I probably got grounded in my belief on the benefits of vacations from my parents. My dad has a Ph.D. in metallurgy and my mom is a medical doctor. Both of them worked extremely hard prior to retirement and were fully committed to their jobs. Still, they never failed to take their vacations. And when they went on vacations, it was truly all about vacation. If it was a family excursion, it was family bonding time. If it was just the two of them, it was time for them to build their relationship and commitment to one another and to catch up on each other's lives. Because both of them worked so hard when they were home, they only did what they had to do to maintain the house, their relationship with each other, and with their children. There are only so many hours in the day and even though both of them loved their work, they needed those vacations, and they took them. They gave themselves a brain break and when they came back they were more capable in their jobs. My mom's patients would say they noticed differences in her. Our relationships with them felt better, and they were more capable of all of the things they needed to do as parents.

They had more energy, more patience, and more compassion, so the time they spent with us was quality time. They weren't distracted. My Mom loves her job so much she doesn't know what she would do without her patients, without her seminars, without setbacks and triumphs at work every day. When she returned from vacation she wasn't saying "Oh my God, back to the daily grind!" She was excited to go back to the hospital. She loved it. But she still knew she had to take her vacations to give her the rest she needed to perform at her best.

Through them, I learned that vacation time is just that, real vacation time, not bringing your work with you. My mom could have been writing prescriptions, looking at files remotely, taking phone calls, and faxing in details. Doctors do it all the time. But she didn't do it because she wanted to be a better doctor for her patients and she needed that downtime so that her brain could recharge and expand.

Vacations bolster your capacity to be fully involved and engaged in your life. You can be your very best you. Without them, it can be like a stream train running on green wood. You can't go as far or as fast, and you run out of steam faster. Unlike a train, if you run out of steam as a person, you can keep chugging, right? You're moving, but you're not working at your best. Learning to take vacations properly can be completely life changing. It can make everything in your life work better.

Vacations are a form of play. There is a spectrum of play as with everything else that I talk about. To play is to engage in activity for enjoyment and recreation rather than for a serious or practical purpose. The characteristics of play all have to do with motivation and mental attitude, not with any actual behavior. Two people might be throwing a ball, or pounding nails, or typing words on a computer, and one might be playing while the other feels like they are working.

Play isn't necessarily all-or-nothing. It can blend with other motives and attitudes, in proportions ranging anywhere from 0% up to 100% pure play. Pure play happens more often in children than in adults. In adults, play is commonly mixed with other motives that usually have to do with adult responsibilities and competitiveness. That is why, in everyday conversation, we tend to talk about children "playing" and adults "being playful" in their activities. We intuitively think of playfulness as being on a spectrum.

There are two characteristics of play:

(1) Play is self-chosen and self-directed.

(2) Play is an activity in which the means are more important than the ends.

Play is an expression of joy and freedom. It is what one *wants* to do as opposed to what one is *obligated* to do. The joy of play is the ecstatic feeling of freedom. It is not always accompanied by smiles and laughter, nor are smiles and laughter always signs of play, but play is always accompanied by a feeling of "Yes, this is what I want to do right now."

Our culture is focused a lot on the mind. Even in personal growth, we are focused on the concept of changing our minds and the way we think. We forget that most of the magic happens in the rest of our beings, and that the mind is only a piece of who we are. It is not all of who we are. We need pause and play for the recharging and the healing of the mind. We also need them for the healing and the rejuvenation of the rest of us because true magic, bliss, happens when we engage our entire bodies. Play is a way to integrate all of you. It is a way to open all of you up so you can have access to all of those parts inside of you that contribute to your life.

Play happens kinesthetically. It bypasses the mind and goes straight to the heart, straight to the body, straight to the spirit. It helps us get in touch with who we are and releases our minds and hearts to experience joy and freedom.

Studies on play have been conducted by many organizations. Two of note are *Play as an Organizing Principle* by John Byers, and *Effective Neuroscience: The Foundation of Human and Animal Emotion* by Jaak Pankseep. Their studies show that play stimulates growth in the amygdala which controls emotions. They also show it promotes pre-fontal cortex development which controls cognition. It makes us more emotionally mature and smarter. It also improves decision making ability.

To play is instinctive, intuitive, and natural. It's the oldest form of learning for humans. As adults we are often trained to think that the opposite of play is work, but that's not true. The opposite of play is depression. Depression creates stagnation and compression. When we are compressed, we are less creative and productive. If you think play is frivolous, realize that you are limiting yourself. You are confining yourself. Consider instead that play could be the most important capability human beings have. And to limit your capability to play is to handicap yourself. If you can't play, you limit your brain power, your productivity, your capacity to connect with others, and your creativity. Most of all, you limit your capacity to dream, to see the impossible and imagine it as possible. You limit your capacity to make those dreams come true. Without the capacity to play, you can't be blissful.

"Bliss doesn't last forever. It's like brushing your teeth, you have to work on it every day."

~ Moneeka Sawyer

Chapter Ten
Setting Up Your
Morning Routine for Bliss

Each morning we are born again. What we do today is wha
matters most."

~ **Buddha**

Over the years, several coaches have tried to convince me of
the importance of establishing a morning routine. I hope you pay
better attention to me than I did to them. Although they insisted
that it was important on a lot of different levels, I didn't get it, and
I didn't practice it. There was a key missing for me, and I would
like to share that with you.

It begins with the subconscious mind, the part of your mind
that controls 97 percent of everything that you do. When you go
into autopilot, even when you are conscious and awake, you are
acting from your subconscious. Your conscious brain is only 3
percent of who you are, even though it is what you are most aware
f. Yet the 97 percent controls all of your bodily functions,
luding the voices in your head that make you do the things you
a conscious person.

rder for you to create change and true bliss in your life you
have the support of the subconscious mind. It needs to
vehicle of change. Yet, in many ways, you should think
erful subconscious mind of yours as a six-year-old
ve to be very literal with it because it doesn't
tract   ideas,   big   words,   or   emotional

consequences. It doesn't really understand right from wrong. It is just like a child who is simply having experiences. When you are trying to communicate with it or to influence it, you can't use the communication techniques that you use as an adult to convince your conscious mind. You can't argue with the subconscious mind on adult terms. You can't reason or rationalize with it. You can't negotiate with it. It doesn't hear the word "no." If you think about it, the negative is an abstract concept, and the subconscious mind doesn't understand abstract concepts.

What does the subconscious mind understand?

- Patterns.
- Images.
- Emotions.
- Repetition of the above.

As you can see, the subconscious is not really keyed into words.

For example, suppose you are trying to come up with an affirmation. If you say "I don't want to be poor," the subconscious only sees an *image* of poor. That's going to point the subconscious towards that image, which is not what you wanted at all. "I would like to be financially free" is too abstract. The subconscious might get an image of you happily spending all your money. "I am very, very safe and comfortable at all times," cr a different *image,* and it creates an emotional response. I the present tense as if you are experiencing it r statements send an image of wanting anotʰ giving your subconscious a picture of a rⁱ

If you've tried affirmations
it's because you're creating
components necessary to co
Maybe you don't have a compⱡ
the emotion behind that image
affirmation over time will create

process. A quicker process is to change patterns and create interruptions in current patterns. That's why the morning routine is so powerful. It is an easy, simple, yet very physical, conscious way to change a pattern. It creates a change in your physical reality, and it also breaks a subconscious pattern. This provides you with more opportunity to feed it good information with new beliefs and patterns.

The morning routine is really about establishing your day-to-day experience and making you feel good consciously and emotionally. It is also about breaking the momentum of a current pattern and opening up your subconscious mind to new information.

Here's an example of my own morning routine.

There are a lot of different things that you can wake up to, and our smartphones are amazing tools for that. They allow you to choose the music that you play to wake you up. No more buzzing alarms of the past. I took it a step farther and recorded affirmations that I want to wake up to, and that's what I hear as my morning alarm.

For a long time, my affirmation was, "I am so very grateful for my amazing life," and my phone repeated that mantra until I turned it off. When I was dancing professionally and needed to lose some weight (and gain some self-confidence), my affirmation was, "I am beautiful, healthy, and fit." It doesn't matter how many times I press snooze. Each time I do, I wake again to an affirmation. You can use whatever affirmation inspires you and change it as often as you like.

Once you wake up, you might do as I do and focus on expressing three things that you are grateful for. (I call these gratitudes.) You can start with something short and easy, just to get in the habit of it.

My gratitudes focus on my life, my work, myself, and sometimes my relationships. Once I do a few quick gratitudes, I doze off again, feeling really good. I think this is the single most important thing I do for my bliss every single day. The topic of gratitude practice is huge, so I won't go into it much here. I will go more into depth about this in the next chapter.

The next time my alarm goes off, I know it's really time to get out of bed. When I sit up, the very first thing that I do is drink a cup of water. If you have slept through the night, your body will have become dehydrated. Drinking a room-temperature glass of water helps to rehydrate and re-energize your body. I place a glass of water by my bedside before I sleep. When I drink it in the morning, it is at room temperature.

I feed the dog and get ready for the day. Finally, my husband and I go out and walk the dog. This gives me some movement in my morning and some family and relationship time. Then we will grab a cup of coffee and walk home before my husband goes to work. If my husband isn't with me, I might do a short walking meditation. In the bliss work I do with my clients, we talk a lot about how movement really cleanses and energizes the body. We'll also discuss this a bit more later in this book. For me, a walking meditation has significantly higher impact than a regular meditation. I recommend that you take the time to have a little bit of space for yourself to get centered, regardless of whether it is a little bit of movement or a little bit of meditation.

My workday usually starts at about ten o'clock. The first thing I do when I sit down at my desk is to search for and read some motivational quotes or look at some short inspiring videos. It makes me smile and starts my working day off right.

I know that it is hard for some people to fathom putting together a morning routine because they are already so rushed and overwhelmed in the morning. If you are one of those people and while reading this you are thinking something like: *I don't have time for all of this. I don't want to do this.* This is stressing me out.

Realize that you already have a morning routine. It may not be conscious or seem like a routine, but we all have a "way" that we start our days. Let's take a look at yours.

- What time do you usually wake up in the morning?
- How many hours of sleep do you usually get?
- How are you awakened and to what?
- What do you do right after you wake up?
- What are all the things you do before you start working?

Take it very, very slowly. Change just a little bit at a time and add just a little bit more of a time commitment. Don't jump in gung ho. Don't announce to yourself or anyone else, "I am going to do this and I am going to take an hour for my morning routine. This is going to be awesome!"

Instead, start with the simple things like changing what you wake up to. Drinking that glass of water I mentioned doesn't take any extra time. If you have a dog, you have to walk him anyway. Instead of stressing over that time you have to spend with your dog, really appreciate that walk. Look at the trees and the flowers around you. Just take the things that you are already doing and maximize them for yourself. You don't need to add time, but you do need to add awareness in order to maximize the benefit for yourself because this is really about you. It is not about anybody else. If you are not being aware, you are robbing yourself.

You might say, "I need that time to look at my phone. That's how I keep up with what I am doing."

Well, have you considered that constantly looking at your phone is probably stressing you out? None of us performs at our best when we are really stressed out, so it is important that you take care of yourself enough that when you do hit the workplace—whatever that is for you—that you can hit the ground running, fully alive, fully aware, and fully present, so you are not frazzled before even getting started in the day.

Most of all, remember that your life is your responsibility and your joy is your responsibility. If the very first thing you do is wake up in the morning and look at what emails need to be handled, you are immediately giving away your power to everybody else.

I worked as a mortgage broker for five years, and a lot of friends who are still in that industry look at their phones first thing in the morning to find out what loan has closed, what client has an emergency, and any number of things. They immediately send their bodies into that fight mode, which then makes them want to flee. They want to run away immediately because they are already stressed. What I really recommend for those people, and for you, is to give yourself a break. I understand there are things that are important and there are days when I also have to look at my email very first thing in the morning because there is something really urgent that needs to be handled. But that is not every day. If you need to plunge into stress every, single, solitary day, it would help you to figure out how to create a productive model that's does not include starting with an emergency every day. Being in constant emergency mode is not the best use of your personal energy and it does not support the kind of production you are capable of.

Why create a morning routine?

1. It sets you up to live the day you want.
2. It sets up the energy and flow of your morning to be more positive.
3. Simple changes have BIG impact.
4. It's easy to change.
5. You are doing it anyway so why not do it consciously?

The demands of life are very real. Some things in your morning you can control, and some you can't. Having a routine set up helps you to remain in your place of calm more easily.

Exercise:

To help you integrate this concept into your life, let's do a quick exercise.

Take a piece of paper and draw a line down the middle of the page.

On the left side of the line answer these questions I mentioned earlier:

- What time do you usually wake up in the morning?
- How many hours of sleep do you usually get?
- How are you awakened and to what?
- What do you do right after you wake up?
- What are all the things you do before you start working?

Being aware of how you are doing things is the first step toward making the changes that will make your life more blissful.

Let's take a look at how we might tweak your morning routine.

1. What is the tone and sound of what you wake up to? Is it a jarring alarm, news, or music? This is when your subconscious is most like a sponge. This time between sleep and waking is when your subconscious is at its most vulnerable. Think about what it is taking in. Change to something soothing, affirming, and kind to your subconscious.
2. What are your first thoughts when you wake up? These should be positive, not negative.
3. Add three gratitudes as your first thoughts. Use life, work and yourself.
4. Add a glass of water to your side table before you go to sleep. It will be at room temperature when you wake up. Drink the entire thing in the morning. It will hydrate your body without sending it into the shock that cold water will.

Now write these things on the right side of you page and add them into your morning routine.

Notice, I haven't asked for a big commitment of your time in the morning. Try this for a week and you will notice your energy levels shifting with each day. See how it affects you happiness levels.

What can you expect?

- To feel more relaxed and happy
- To have creative surges
- To be less agitated throughout the day and feel more grounded
- To feel more at peace and ....ah....bliss

At the end of the week write down what shifts you have noticed. Continue to adjust your morning routine until you love it. This isn't iron clad. Life changes, and you will need to shift it again. That's okay. Just stay conscious of your morning routine and make sure it is always serving you.

Chapter Eleven
The Secret Behind the Power of Gratitude

"Gratitude can transform common days into thanksgivings, turn routine jobs into joy, and change ordinary opportunities into blessings."

~ **William Arthur Ward**

I consider gratitude the master skill of bliss. It is the one skill that can have the biggest impact on people's lives with the least amount of effort. Who doesn't like that? It impacts everything – life, love, work, prosperity, and contentment.

Let's define gratitude. There is a whole spectrum of gratitude. On the lower end of the spectrum there is the feeling of thanks that comes when someone does something nice for you or gives you something. This form of gratitude is really good, but it's a short-term feeling of thanks. The operative words here are short-term. On the other end of the spectrum, a grateful person habitually looks at life from a grateful focus. They have a deep abiding sense of thankfulness for life as a fundamental life orientation. Although it's good to express thanks no matter where you are on this spectrum, the more time you spend in the deeper part of that spectrum, the more you will experience the benefits of being a truly grateful person.

I'm sure you have heard a lot about gratitude over the last few years. It's a hot topic. But how many of you have developed your own gratitude practices? Many of us haven't. We know intuitively that gratitude is important to our well-being, and it makes us feel good, so why don't we make it a priority in our lives?

There are many reasons why. First, maybe we're not completely convinced that it's important. Our heart knows it's important, but our brain may not be convinced.

Second, maybe it feels like "just another thing to add to our schedule," and we just don't have the energy to do it.

Third, maybe we've tried it in the past and it hasn't given us the results we were hoping for.

These are just a few of the many reasons why we don't add a gratitude practice into our lives. I'll address these first and we'll talk about a few other obstacles later.

To address the first issue, let's get our brains onboard with how important gratitude is to our well-being. There have been many studies on the benefits of gratitude, but I particularly like one that has been conducted at UC Davis for the past 11 years. Approximately 3000-4000 people between the ages of 18 and 80 have gone through the study, and the research has shown very interesting results. As it turns out, an attitude of gratitude affects all parts of our lives.

Physically: People exercise up to 33% more and feel stronger and better about their exercise. They sleep 10-15% more and they are more refreshed when they wake up. They have less aches and pains, and there are specific studies that show that having a gratitude practice reduces blood pressure, strokes, heart attacks, and hyper-tension.

Psychologically: Gratitude makes people feel more awake, alive, enthusiastic, motivated, and energetic.

Socially: Gratitude makes people feel closer to others and more connected. They are more helpful and feel more loving, giving, forgiving, compassionate, and humble. And other people notice. In the studies, family members of the participants mentioned how much nicer and more helpful the participant was being now that they are practicing gratitude.

Spiritually: Gratitude makes people feel inspired, creative, and fulfilled. They have more open minds and more positive behaviors. They express more positive emotions and when they experience negative emotions, they pull out from them more quickly. Grateful people feel and are perceived as more mature.

Gratitude helps us to celebrate the present and engage more fully in life because it magnifies the positive. It blocks toxic emotions, especially with regard to jealousy, resentment, regret, and depression. It makes people more stress-resilient. Gratitude is an ally in our struggles with negativity and negative events. It makes us more resilient when we are struggling with trauma, adversity, suffering, or anxiety. It helps us come back to a more positive interpretation of life events when we recount the event in the future. Our memories no longer weigh us down with resentment, anger, bitterness, helplessness, or other negative emotions. We are lighter and free to experience our lives with more joy and bliss.

I have been doing gratitude work for about 15 years. It has transformed my life in such a positive way that I talk about it often. It's interesting to me that some people object to it.

I've been told that being grateful is selfish and immature. According to this idea, if I'm grateful, I am obviously not aware of all the suffering and trauma that is happening in the world. To that, I ask people what being aware of those things does for them. Are they doing anything about it? In my experience when someone is filled up inside with love, joy and gratitude, they feel safe and taken care of. From that place they are able to help others in need. A grateful person acknowledges that there is suffering, scarcity, and trauma in the world, but they are able to help instead of getting depressed about it. They are leaders in doing socially responsible work in industry, and doing good for their families, friends, and communities. They are more compassionate, generous, charitable, and forgiving.

In their own lives, when they themselves suffer, they are able to bounce back faster. And they problem solve more creatively to lift themselves out of their situation and emotional state more quickly.

Another thing people say is "If I'm so grateful, how will I be motivated to succeed at anything?" People seem to think that gratitude will make them lazy or complacent. "If I'm grateful for everything I have, why would I work for more?"

Studies, and my personal experience, have shown that grateful people actually do and accomplish more that less grateful people. They feel energized and happy. They are more creative and playful. They naturally take more vigorous action more often. They are statistically higher achievers than their less-grateful counterparts.

Yet another thing people say is "Moneeka, it's really hard to be grateful when things are so bad." Yes, suffering is a huge obstacle to gratefulness. But if you are a person who has developed a grateful disposition you will be more resilient through difficult times. You'll pull out of it faster, be able to problem solve to fix issues more easily, and you won't fall as low emotionally as you might have otherwise.

Finally, I hear "I've done a lot of gratitude practices and either I wasn't able to stick with them, or they didn't give me the results I wanted."

Would you like one hint on how to make gratitude practices more effective in your life? You need to make sure that when you say, think, or write your thoughts of gratitude you do it in a way that invokes emotion.

This chapter is called the secret behind the power of gratitude. The secret that I'm talking about is *feeling* gratitude. It's the feeling that will keep you uplifted. Our thoughts, words, and actions all help us to attain and maintain that feeling. It's that feeling that gives us all the benefits that I've stated above.

Exercise:

Let's do a quick gratitude exercise together. Take out a journal and write down three things you are grateful for. If you have a hard time thinking of three, use the structure of giving one gratitude each for your life, your work, and yourself. So what this might sound like is:

For my life: I am so grateful to have a sweet little dog that shows me unconditional love and makes me laugh all the time.

For my work: I'm so grateful that I get to work every day with people I love, admire, and respect.

For myself: I'm so grateful that I have been blessed with the strength to keep plugging away at things even when I'm tired.

Take a moment to do this now.

That was easy right? That's a great start and if that's all you do every day, just three gratitudes, it will greatly impact your life. Remember to get the most impact out of your practice, it's the emotion behind the gratitude that makes your practice powerful. It's that feeling that elevates all the pieces of your life. It's hard to evoke the feeling when you are not feeling good. However, we also need to do our gratitude practice when we are feeling good. It's important that we develop a practice that becomes an automatic part of our life so it can help lift us out of the bad times and help us stay in the good times longer.

An easy way to start a gratitude practice is to keep a gratitude journal. This is the gratitude practice most of us hear a lot about and was used for all the studies I did research on. Start a journal in which you write 3-5 gratitudes every morning and every night. Remember to take the time to really feel the gratitudes as you write them down. I have to admit, I personally have not been able to stick with a gratitude journal. I love the idea and really encourage people to keep one, but for me, I just haven't been able to be consistent with it.

I had to come up with some other things to do. I'm going to share my practices here, but I'd like you to use your own creativity and imagination to come up with a practice that will work best for you.

I think three gratitudes in the morning after I push the snooze button on my alarm. This sets my day up to be very joyful. The secret to the success of this practice is that I don't just state the gratitudes and move on. I know I mentioned in my morning routine chapter to say them quickly without spending too much time on them. But as you get more accustomed to doing them, I'd deepen the practice a little bit. What I do is state the gratitude and then expand on it. I'm trying to connect to the core positive feelings for each of the things I am grateful for.

For instance, instead of saying "I am so grateful for my beautiful home." I might say something like "I am so grateful for my beautiful home because it makes me feel safe, secure, stable, loved and warm."

What I'd like you to try in your gratitude practice is to say what you are grateful for and then give a reason that is emotion based. Express the emotions you attach to that thing that you are grateful for. This will make your gratitude practice much stronger.

I also think three gratitudes every night just before I go to sleep. I do this in the same way as I do my morning gratitudes and it sets me up to have a pleasant night's sleep and to wake up feeling positive and happy.

Let's practice this concept now. Take out your journal and write three gratitudes in the way I just described. Write down the gratitude and the emotions associated with that gratitude.

I might say, "I am so grateful for my beautiful office in my home. It makes me feel relaxed, secure, and energized. It's a place where I can focus on what is important to me. The sayings around the room inspire and uplift me. I love the squirrels that run up the tree outside my window because they make me giggle and remind me to have fun. I feel so blessed to have such a beautiful place to do my work in every single day."

Does that make sense? Now it's your turn. Take a minute to try it right now.

How did that feel? Continue this practice for a week. If you have trouble thinking of some gratitudes to say, try giving one gratitude for your life, work, and yourself. Regarding the gratitude about yourself, please remember that we are trying to be kind to ourselves. It's not about being prideful or arrogant. We are just trying to acknowledge what is beautiful about ourselves. Let's be grateful for what our gifts are, what we appreciate about ourselves and what we are able to give back to the world.

Another idea you might try is a gratitude bracelet. This bracelet can really be anything you wear. It provides a physical cue to remind you to think or say a gratitude in any moment that you happen to look at it.

You can use other physical cues also. I have a client who has decided that every single time she sees a stop sign instead of getting frustrated that it's slowing her down, she says a gratitude.

What about a gratitude shower? I have a friend with a rock in his shower with the word gratitude etched into it. As he showers with that warm, cleansing water flowing over him, he says five gratitudes and feels the emotions attached to them.

Can technology help us out here? I have set up gratitude alarms on my phone. I set the alarms to go off at different times of the day and when I look at my screen to shut off the alarm it says "I am so grateful for…." And I finish the statement spontaneously in that moment.

Whenever you are doing a gratitude practice try deepening it this way.

1. When you are cued to do a gratitude, take a couple long deep breaths and get really present in your body.
2. Say the gratitude with feeling.
3. Express the emotions associated with that gratitude.
4. Take another deep cleansing breath to settle into those yummy feelings.

If you can't do all the steps, don't worry about it. Just saying the gratitude is great.

There are two more practices I think really increase the feeling of gratitude in people's lives. First, do something good for someone else. The act of being kind and giving to someone you love, a stranger, or to your community just makes you feel good. It makes you feel grateful that you have the resources to be helpful and kind. It kindles all kinds of self-appreciation, gratitude, and compassion inside of you. Giving something to someone else takes you outside of yourself. It helps you to think of others and you stop focusing so much on what might not be so great in your own life.

The last practice I want to mention is to send out regular gratitude messages. I will often send out a text, email, or card to someone saying thank you for "just being you" and for being such a beautiful part of my life. It makes my day and it definitely makes theirs also, so it's a serious win-win.

I consider gratitude to be the master skill of bliss. Develop a practice you love, and your life will never be the same.

Chapter Twelve
Movement Is Bliss

"When movement is experienced as joy, it adorns our lives, makes our days better, and gives us something to look forward to. It may even inspire us to do things we never thought possible."

~ Scott-Kretchmer
Professor of Exercise and Sport Science at Penn State

Just the act of moving, even if it is just ten or twenty minutes a day, solves so many of my personal problems, physical and emotional. It will do the same for you.

From the time I was very young, any time music would come on I'd start to move and dance. It was a normal thing to do for me. By the time I was three, I was always up and dancing to music. My mom and dad realized my passion and put me into dance classes when I was five years old. I've continued to love dance my entire life. It has always been one of those stabilizing forces to me. I used to dance six hours a day when I was in high school because I performed often, specializing in Bharatanatyam, which is a classical Indian style of dance.

I had not known until I was in my twenties what life would be like without dance.

It was moving day.

My white Geo Prizm was packed with all my belongings—full

of boxes and clothes, as much as I could fit for this trip to my new apartment. I was on my way to Santa Clara, excited about what was ahead.

It was rush hour, and I was on the main drag, San Thomas Expressway, five lanes in one direction, barely moving. I didn't mind. I turned up the radio and sang along to "Forever Young," enjoying the adventure.

I was three cars back from the stoplight. Stopped. Waiting. Singing along.

Without warning, my car imploded.

I heard the screech of tires and the sound of metal crumpling. As my dashboard was pushed back into my chest, the rear of my car propelled me forward. My body was crushed as the car compacted like an accordion, glass exploding everywhere around me. If it were not for the boxes packed in tight behind me, I don't know if I would have survived.

Somehow, in a daze, I pushed my door open and got out of the car. I began picking up my belongings that were strewn around the street as the cars around me moved down the street.

"Honey. Honey! You need to stop." Some woman had pulled over and approached me.

"No, no. Just one more thing," I said, barely coherent, blood trickling down my cheek.

She kindly ran out and grabbed whatever treasure I had pointed at, then guided me to the curb.

When the fire trucks arrived, a fireman sat down next to me and started asking me questions. I was in such shock, I couldn't speak.

"Do you know where you are? Do you know your name?"

I just nodded.

"Sweetie, please don't move your head." Later I learned that they were afraid I had broken my neck.

I nodded again. He held my head between his hands and asked me another question.

I couldn't talk. I started to cry.

While the fireman was still trying to get me to respond, the driver of the white Cadillac that rear-ended me approached.

"When are we going to be done with this?" he said. "I didn't need this tonight. I'm already late for a date with my fiancée."

When I arrived at the hospital, I still hadn't found my voice, so no one had been contacted or even knew what had happened to me.

Eventually, I woke up to see my brother at my bedside. I was in a haze from all the painkillers. Now that I was awake, the doctor came in to tell me about my condition.

"Your legs have been seriously damaged. They aren't broken, but both your hips are dislocated, and your knees are terribly swollen. We're not sure how you're going to recover, and you'll never be able to walk the same again."

The doctor said that they were ordering me a wheelchair and that I'd be incapacitated for a while.

"What's the process for getting me out of the wheelchair?" I asked, fighting to comprehend what he was telling me.

"We'll figure that out later. For now, we just want to manage your pain."

"Absolutely not," I said. "We're going to figure this out without a wheelchair."

I was bound and determined to walk again. Not only that, but I had danced for seventeen years, and I was going to dance again.

Within two months, I was able to endure being upright, either sitting or standing, for an hour or two at a time. After six months, I was finally able to "walk," which actually meant shuffle around, usually holding onto something. But even after two years of being on significant pain medication and ongoing physical therapy, the constant pain had still not gone away. Sitting was extremely painful, and at night, I would go to bed crying.

If I didn't take the drugs, I couldn't sleep. If I took the drugs, I couldn't function. My brain would be all muddled. And after two years, the medication I was taking was eating me up on the inside. I was searching for an alternative and met an acupuncturist who said he could help me. Once I started acupuncture, the pain became manageable in only three months. After six months, I went off pain medication. Although the pain was still constant, I made progress, and I could really walk. Maybe, I told myself, I would be able to dance again one day.

Because I wasn't dancing I put on a great deal of weight. I also became depressed, not only because of the weight gain, but because I couldn't exercise, and the level of mind-uplifting endorphins that my body was used to were absent.

The constant pain affected my personality dramatically. At the time—long before I met my husband—I was engaged to someone else, and because of the changes my fiancé and I started arguing. A lot of really horrible things happened between us, and eventually we broke up.

In addition, because of the pain, I wasn't able to keep up with my work. I changed jobs three times in three years. The accident had not just affected me physically. It had ripped my entire life apart.

I couldn't move. I couldn't get out of bed. I was paralyzed.

This wasn't physical. Sure, the car accident had ruined my legs and displaced my hips. But my true paralysis was from depression.

Even after I married Dave, as my career changes piled up,

friends and family couldn't understand what was wrong. It started with helpful suggestions and in time became criticism and exasperation. Subtle and not-so-subtle whispers of disapproval entered conversations around me.

There was this perception that I couldn't hold a job and was just a loser living off my husband's money. Because I didn't complain about it, people didn't seem to understand how much pain I was in, and what that was doing to me. People even told David that he could do so much better, and that he should leave me and marry someone of his caliber.

I felt the daily strain of this criticism but was determined to live my life the way I wanted to live it. To make it worse, I had the daily pain—the physical pain—that came from the car crash.

Over time, I started to feel a lifetime of criticism for my decisions, and that began to paralyze me. I fell into a deep depression. I realized that I had been criticized my entire life for my choices, and I felt I was never going to be accepted. I began to believe I was never going to be successful.

I gave up. The criticism won the battle. I just wanted the pain to end. I couldn't just keep "being positive" anymore. Nothing I did was working. Between the physical pain of the car crash and the emotional pain of being criticized for not having a career, I felt hopeless. Despair took over my life.

My depression lasted for more than three years.

Many times, I thought about the relief of just ending it all.

During this time, I let go of any hopes of a career. I went on anti-depressants and saw all different kinds of therapists. I was searching for answers about what was wrong with me and how I could fix it. The anti-depressants numbed the pain, but after a while, I realized that I wasn't feeling anything. I wasn't feeling pain, but I wasn't feeling joy, love, excitement, or any kind of bliss either. I realized that I didn't want to live my life numbed out. I wanted to feel alive again. I had to find a way to be happy, and a way that was without the drugs.

I went off the medication and spent another year basically sleeping, crying, and searching. During this time, I dug deeply into my soul for the answers I so desperately needed.

I didn't dance for six years after the car accident. Traditional Indian dance—what I had danced my entire life—was out of the question. It was too percussive, too demanding. Instead, I began dancing again with hula. It was gentle and fluid, and the pain I experienced was minimal.

Returning to dance—any form of dance—was like rediscovering my soul again. After the car crash and being unable to walk normally for so long, hula dancing helped me get back my balance and equilibrium. I felt graceful again.

But after four years of dancing hula, I found myself wanting something different. It was then that I discovered Alyne, a belly dance instructor.

"I need you to understand that I have really bad legs and hips," I explained. "I can't do anything percussive."

"We won't do anything that will hurt you or cause you pain," Alyne assured me. "We'll listen to your body, and you will dance."

I began private lessons right away and focused on what was for me a new expression of dance: veil work. I fell madly in love with it.

"You're so lucky," Alyne said one day after our session together.

"What?!"

"You're so lucky," she repeated. "The reason you'll be such a good veil dancer is because you've had to relearn how your body works—how your legs work, and how your arms work. Most adults don't have this awareness and don't know what they are capable of doing."

I was stunned into silence. She made it seem like my accident was actually a good thing. I had never even considered that a possibility.

Dance gave me my life back, the life that I wanted. I was able to move again. I started to lose weight. I had those endorphins going through my body. The movement was helping to re-lubricate my joints, so we could figure out which pain was just from not moving and which pain really had to be dealt with. I could deal with the pain through holistic means instead of having to turn to painkillers.

There was so much more that became possible once I was moving again. Even now, I still have a low level of pain all of the time, but I function like a perfectly normal person. I can still dance two or three hours in a row, five days a week. I can still walk. I can stand for a long period of time and I can drive. Without movement, I felt dead. With movement, I'm able to be fully alive on all levels.

I think my story is proof that movement is important.

When I convince my clients to take even a ten-minute walk after dinner, they tell me how much better they feel. It aids digestion, sleep, and overall well-being, and it's only ten minutes.

You just have to take that first step. Even if you walk five minutes one way, turn around and walk five minutes back.

There are days when my body refuses to cooperate. There are still those days when it is painful for me to get out of the bed. Thankfully they are very infrequent, but on those days I still get up. I put on a five minutes stopwatch on my phone and I walk five minutes away and five minutes back. It is amazing how the pain goes down so quickly. Because I just moved a little bit, I got my body used to being vertical and functioning. Now, before I take a painkiller, I always go for a little five- or ten-minute round-trip walk just to see if I was just feeling stiffness instead of pain.

If you don't already exercise, add it in gently to your life. If you are in a class, be aware of your body. If an exercise is really hurting, if you feel something snap, or if you feel like you are being pushed too hard, back off. No matter what the instructor says, you be aware of your body and what you need.

Exercise with other people is awesome. Just don't get caught up in the natural inclination to be competitive with the people you are exercising with. Be true to yourself, stopping when it is enough, and honoring what you can do today.

If you honor what you can do right now, then you get to exercise some more tomorrow and the next day. But if you don't honor what you are capable of today and you hurt yourself, you will not be able to progress tomorrow.

A study done by doctors at the University of Texas medical center, found that people who exercise for 30 minutes a day every day are almost half as likely to be depressed as people who do not exercise. Exercise also increases alpha brain wave activity. That's the brain wave that helps you clear your mind and focus.

So, learn to take care of yourself. You don't need to be a model, marathon runner, or professional athlete. Just don't neglect your health.

It starts with one step in the right direction. If you already have some kind of exercise you love, do that more consistently. I'm going to give you a journaling assignment later in this chapter. You can do the journaling for any form of exercise you choose.

I know there are lots of excuses to not exercise. It might be overwhelming to add yet another thing into our schedule. Your body may hurt. Maybe you're too tired. Or there are too many other things you feel you should be doing.

I'd like you to consider how important exercise is to your well-being and commit to just trying a little exercise this week. And for the purposes of this chapter I'm going to suggest doing yoga.

Why Yoga?

Oxford University found that people who practice Yoga even once a week were less stressed, had lower blood pressure, and slept better at night.

According to the national institute of health, yoga is proven to help with muscular skeletal issues, especially lower back pain. It can even help to relieve asthma.

Some people think it's too difficult. There are many types of yoga. While some do promote straining hard, others are gentler.

Pranayama yoga focuses on deep breathing and gentle stretching. This is the yoga that the researchers at Oxford studied and found to be so intricately connected to happiness. Anyone at any skill level can try pranayama.

Here's a twenty-minute exercise:

Stand comfortably, evenly on your two feet.

(Have your weight distributed evenly from your heels to your toes.).

Center yourself, and notice your breath.

Breathe deeply. Try to stay away from shallow upper chest breathing.

Slow down that breath and see if you can breathe into your belly.

Allow the belly to fill up like a balloon. And when you release the breath, feel your belly deflate like a balloon would.

Take a few minutes just to focus on your breath.

Now, when you breathe in, raise your arms in a slow motion above your head.

And when you breathe out, lower your arms.

Keep your shoulders down, and relax your hands.

Repeat raising and lowering your arms as you breathe.

This is very simple, but it's really good stuff.

You can do this for as long as you like.

If this is too simple you can look up something that is a little bit more involved.

Search the web for "sun salutation" or a beginner's yoga sequence.

If you are already familiar with yoga, are you doing it? If not, try to get back to it. As I mentioned earlier, if you don't like yoga, add some exercise you do enjoy into your weekly schedule.

Exercise:

Here is your journaling activity:

In your journal take stock of how you feel after you exercise.

1. How did you feel before your exercise?
2. Was it hard to get started?
3. What worries were you focusing on that day?
4. How did you feel during the exercise?
5. How did you feel after the exercise?
6. How does your breathing feel now?
7. Do you notice a difference in your posture?
8. Do you notice any changes in your mood?
9. Do you feel more focused?

Try doing ten minutes of exercise every day for a week. See how you feel at the end of the week and write down how your mood has changed in that period. Did you feel more focused? The brain recognizes success when it sees it. Which means, the better you feel emotionally after working out, the more likely you are to do it on a regular basis.

You'll reap all the physical benefits too: more flexibility, better muscle tone, less pain, and lots more energy and vitality. Soon your body will be supporting your bliss in a whole new way.

Chapter Thirteen
The Gift of Helping Others

"If you want happiness...

For an hour - take a nap

For a day - go fishing For a

month - get married For a

year - inherit a fortune

For a lifetime - help somebody else."

~ **Chinese Proverb**

Notice the wisdom of this old proverb. The first two things are momentary pleasures. They make you happy for a short time and are fleeting. Getting married and inheriting a fortune are major circumstantial changes in life, but people adapt to circumstantial changes over time, so they no longer have the effect on us that they had in the beginning. As humans, we get used to a new level of happiness or wealth and start to take it for granted. Adaptation is part of human nature, and this ability to adapt to change is a very important part of us.

Helping others is a conscious action. In most cultures, there is the concept that helping others means you are a good person. If you see yourself that way, you have a healthier self-perception. It builds self-esteem. You see yourself as interconnected to others, which is a very important factor to people's happiness. The feeling of being alone depresses people. The feeling of being connected to others and being part of a larger whole is in our DNA and a very important contributor to being happy.

Two studies I looked at, one from Simon Fraser University in Canada and one from UC Riverside, show that helping others improves your happiness and well-being. The studies asked participants to do five random acts of kindness a day for six weeks. They found that doing this consistently, dramatically increased happiness because it shifts us from self-centeredness to other centeredness.

(This research was published in the Journal of Experimental Social Psychology.)

It makes us feel connected and it relieves distress and discomfort we feel over other people's misfortunes.

Yet it seems the biggest benefit in helping others are the social consequences. You can make new friends. Other people appreciate what you've done, so you feel recognized. They, in turn, may reciprocate. Helping others leads to a cascade of positive social consequences that contribute to a person's happiness.

When you start to help others and see yourself as good, you are more likely to see good in others. That helps you to feel better about the world which, in turn, makes you feel happier.

The studies also suggested that more happiness is experienced if the act of doing something kind for others requires a level of personal sacrifice. There is a concept known as "giver's high." We get this feeling anytime we help others, but we feel it more deeply if we have had to give something up to help someone else. Whether it was time, an object, whatever. If we made a personal sacrifice we experience a higher high.

We feel happiness more if it involved personal interaction. We feel a giver's high when we give money to a cause for sure, but we feel it more when we help someone in a way that we can see them react.

We feel more abundant if we are able to help someone else. It allows you to see how much you actually do have and to feel grateful for it. Helping others improves our perspective on life.

Giving makes you more compassionate toward the needs of others. Of course, making other people smile naturally makes us feel good too.

If you look around, you'll see random acts of kindness big and small. From holding open a door for someone, to helping build houses in other countries, there are so many things that we can do to make a contribution.

Helping others doesn't have to be huge. When we think about charity, we often think of, for instance, the Bill Gates Foundation that gives huge amounts of money to help with growth in Third World countries. We may think of Angelina Jolie and Brad Pitt adopting many children from underdeveloped countries. We might think that only the rich can provide help that will affect change, but that's not true. Everything that each of us does, no matter how small, is a step in the right direction to creating a better world for us to live in.

When you are looking at ways to give, don't get stuck on what you are hearing, or what people's perception of giving is. There are many different ways to give, and it can be with your talents as well as your money. It doesn't even need to be outside of your own neighborhood.

When I was in a grocery store parking lot recently, I saw an older woman pushing a cart with a cane hanging from it. Suddenly, the cart got away from her. She couldn't walk without her cane, so she certainly was not going to be able to catch that cart!

I pulled over, jumped out of my car, grabbed the cart before it hit something, and then walked her and the cart to her car. Helping her was not a big deal. She was just someone in need, and it was an opportunity for me to help.

Another time, I was in Germany at a beer festival. It was a beautiful day. People were dancing in the town square. Then unexpectedly it began to rain hard. This often happens in Europe. Everybody scurried for cover, leaving one old man sitting in the center of the square. He was at a table unable to move. I realized he was going to get drenched. I had a coat, so I put my hood on, ran out there with my umbrella and put it over him. I can still remember the way that his eyes welled up with tears of gratitude. What it did for me was more than it did for him.

It was just an umbrella. I didn't make a big world change, but I did make a world of change for me. When you get in the habit of thinking about somebody other than yourself, then your desire to help more grows. You can then do more and give more.

As you know, I am involved in the building and running of a school for poor children in India. At the school, we have people who donate their time to put together the computer systems for the administration and the classrooms. We have people who volunteer their time to put together a curriculum. There are still others who serve the children food. There was one instance when I was in India where they lost all the cooks and all the drivers. We don't even know what happened. Still, volunteers came in, cooked and served the food, and others drove the school buses. I volunteer my time and talents to do fundraising and raise awareness about the school.

I love being involved in this organization and doing this work because it feels like I'm making a big difference in the lives of those children. Without the help of the charity, their futures would be limited beyond belief. I love helping make people's dreams come true. In many cases, these children wouldn't have been able to have dreams if it weren't for the school.

Remember that we are a community on this planet, and we need each other. To give to each other is also to give to ourselves. That's how we love each other.

Start in your own world. What things can you do in your regular day-to-day life? If someone drops something, bend over to pick it up. Give a seat to someone. How about just smiling warmly at someone walking by? Answer your phone as if you're happy to be answering it.

Look a little outside the boundaries of your regular life. Maybe help someone learn to read and write. There are Big Brothers and Big Sisters programs everywhere. Volunteer at a local school.

Start small, and if you feel inspired, move out from there. Helping others can be doing something kind in the moment. It can be volunteering some of your time to help with a project. It can be donating money to help a family member, friend, stranger, or a cause.

Start somewhere. If you think you must do something big, you will never start focusing on giving. Everything starts by taking those first little steps.

I'd like to leave you with a challenge.

Try doing five acts of kindness each and every day for a week. That's easy, isn't it? Keep doing it for another week and for another week, until you have done it for six weeks. In your journal write down how you feel about this challenge before you get started. Write down how you feel personally and how you feel about the challenge at the end of each seven-day period. Watch how things change for you. You'll be amazed at what you see in your life.

Chapter Fourteen
Beyond Authenticity

"The need to leave a legacy is our spiritual need to have a sense of meaning, purpose, personal congruence and contribution."

~ **Stephen Covey**

It seems these days that everyone is telling you that you need to be "authentic." Authenticity is one of the new buzzwords. Let's examine what it means and then move beyond it—to bliss.

What I have presented in this book is some wisdom that can help you to move toward the life that you really want. I hope that this book has shown you the importance of choosing bliss and that it has also given you the tools so that every single day you *can* choose bliss.

Mahatma Gandhi said, "True happiness is when what you say, what you do, and what you think are all the same." We forget that in order to really be happy we have to be congruent. If you are saying or doing something on the outside and thinking something else on the inside, it throws you into a state of emotional flux. Maybe it makes you feel like you are a fraud and you fear that you are going to get found out. Maybe you regret actions you took or things you said because they didn't express your true intentions. There are all sorts of emotional consequences and ramifications to being incongruent.

Being aligned, being authentic, is really just being congruent.

We might have been conditioned by our religion, culture, or family, to look, think, or act a certain way. We are afraid that if we don't do that, we will lose love, be cast out, and be all alone.

We have all sorts of fears about what people will think of us if we express our authentic selves. That's why it can be easy to get incongruent. Our false fronts feel like protection. We may even try to hide our true nature from ourselves, to pretend the false front is really who we are.

The ultimate in bliss is to go beyond just *being* authentic. It is to truly *accept* your authentic self. It is being congruent, aligning all parts of you into one cohesive whole. It's about being fully you and accepting yourself completely. You can achieve some degree of bliss without accepting your authentic self. However, you can never experience the boundless bliss that is available to you unless you do. To accept yourself is to truly love yourself. To truly love yourself is to experience the purest form of bliss.

Now it's up to you. It's your turn to go beyond authenticity, and choose bliss.

Please Review This Book

If you enjoyed reading this book, please take a moment to give it a review. Your review will help more people achieve bliss in their own lives. You can write your review by going to this link:

https://www.amazon.com/dp/B01IAWXIA8/

Special gift

As a thank you for buying and reading my book, I am making available a **bonus chapter** only to those who have read this and are committing their lives to bliss. It's **about using your sexual energy to support and attract more bliss in your life.** If you'd like a copy, go to:

www.coreblisslife.com/bonuschapter/

Discover how to live your life with the freedom to be yourself and live your life your way...With Grace & Ease.

Everyone wants to be happy, but at the same time we seem to struggle with where to find it, or to even understand what it is. The fact is each of us has the capacity to carry and enjoy a great deal of happiness. The problem is that we haven't created a space for it to show up in our lives. We must eliminate the clutter that makes us feel anxious, worried and dissatisfied, and intentionally pursue those things that fill our hearts with joy and contentment. I call this enduring joy and contentment Bliss. With the implementation of a few strategies highlighted in this 4 week program, your personal bliss can be more readily found.

A client of mine, named Ted, had become really discontent with his work. He was a software programmer and was very ambitious so he climbed the corporate ladder to become a manager. Once he got there he couldn't figure out why he was so unhappy. His wife said he'd changed and was a really grumpy guy to live with. After taking this course he discovered that his true passion was to create. Although he enjoyed his team, as a manager he was no longer creating a product and programming it into fruition. So, his passions were being ignored. He spoke to upper management and they transfered him to a position as a project lead, so he could design a product and start to computer program again. Everything changed for him. He became much happier and content, and his productivity skyrocketed. And, his

Did you love "Choose Bliss" and want to know where to go from here?

Do you want specific actionable steps you can take now to make your life more blissful immediately?

Secrets of true Happiness Revealed!

Are you tired of pursuing happiness and not ever really finding it?

Do you have moments of happiness, but they don't last?

marriage got back on track again because he was a more blissful person inside. He was so impressed with how dramatically his whole life turned around, once he prioritized living his Bliss.

In this enlightening and educational training you will discover...

- What bliss is for you and how to have it in your life consistently.
- The top 3 things that are clouding their bliss.
- How to eliminate negativity and start healing any lingering sadness
- How to custom design their own happy life – not just a few fleeting moments
- A surprising way to find happiness, anywhere at any time

Discovering your own unique form of bliss sets you up for success in every area of life.

When you are in alignment and living your bliss, you experience:

1. More joy, passion, and enthusiasm in everything you do.
2. An acceptance of all parts of yourself so you have the freedom to be yourself and live your life your way.
3. Ability to make better decisions to support and nurture bliss in your life.
4. More success in your work, relationships, and life goals.

And it all starts NOW.

Join me for **Choose Bliss: Finally Live a Life of Happiness and Contentment** so you can live life on your terms.

Now, let me be clear...this training is not a magic pill or a silver bullet. Anything worth doing requires effort and commitment. If you don't want to put in the effort needed to lead a more fulfilling, successful, and authentic life, then this won't work for you.

BUT if you seriously want happiness, contentment, passion, and success in your life, **this training is the key.**

Register NOW to find your bliss and live the life that you truly desire.

Go to: http://coreblisslife.com/choose-bliss-happiness/

And because you bought this book, you get a special discount on the course. Just use the code **choosebliss** at check-out.

With Love,

Moneeka

P.S. If there's anyone in your life who could use more clarity and a new sense of direction, then PLEASE share this page with them. You'll be doing them a HUGE favor.

Resources

I'd like to share with you some resources I mentioned in this book. I hope you'll look into them as you follow your own path to bliss.

Badarikashrama Vidyashala (the school I am working with in India)

http://badarikashrama.com/index.php/india-center/vidyashala/

The URL of my blog regarding the school: **www.ProjectTeachAChild.com/home/**.

And of course, my website: **www.CoreBlissLife.com**.

Come to my website to find out about programs I offer, sign up to be live on *Bliss Bits* (my radio program), or to read blog posts about how to bring bliss into your life every day.

About the Author

Moneeka Sawyer has often been described as one of the most joyful people you will ever meet. She personally finds her bliss through helping people live the life of their dreams filled with meaning, purpose, and joy. She's dedicated her life to this calling for the past eleven years and says they have been the best years of her life. She shares her life and her joy with her wonderful husband, David, and adorable Pomeranian in Mountain View, CA.